Ancient American
POETS

Bilingual Press/Editorial Bilingüe

Publisher
　Gary D. Keller

Executive Editor
　Karen S. Van Hooft

Associate Editors
　Brian Ellis Cassity
　Cristina de Isasi
　Linda St. George Thurston

Editorial Board
　Juan Goytisolo
　Francisco Jiménez
　Mario Vargas Llosa

Address:
　Bilingual Press
　Hispanic Research Center
　Arizona State University
　PO Box 875303
　Tempe, Arizona 85287-5303
　(480) 965-3867

ANCIENT AMERICAN POETS

THE FLOWER SONGS OF NEZAHUALCOYOTL

THE SONGS OF DZITBALCHE

THE SACRED HYMNS OF PACHACUTI

*Translated from Nahuatl, Maya, and Quechua
with Lives of the Poets and Introductions by*

JOHN CURL

Bilingual Press/Editorial Bilingüe
TEMPE, ARIZONA

© 2005 by Bilingual Press/Editorial Bilingüe

All rights reserved. No part of this publication may be reproduced or transmitted in any form or by any means, electronic or mechanical, including photocopy, recording, or any information storage and retrieval system, without permission in writing from the publisher, except in the case of brief quotations embodied in critical articles and reviews.

ISBN 1-931010-21-8

Library of Congress Cataloging-in-Publication Data

Ancient American poets / [translated and compiled by] John Curl.
    p. cm.
    Includes bibliographical references.
    In Nahuatl, Maya, and Huanca with parallel English translations.
    ISBN 1-931010-21-8
    1. Nahuatl poetry—Translations into English. 2. Maya poetry—Translations into English. 3. Quechua poetry—Translations into English. I. Curl, John.

PM4068.65.E6A53 2003
897—dc22

                                      2003057848

PRINTED IN THE UNITED STATES OF AMERICA

Front cover art: El alacrán *(1998) by René H. Arceo*

Cover and interior design by John Wincek, Aerocraft Charter Art Service

Acknowledgments

This publication is supported by the Arizona Commission on the Arts with funding from the State of Arizona and the National Endowment for the Arts.

Contents

Preface vii
About These Translations ix

THE FLOWER SONGS OF NEZAHUALCOYOTL   1
ANCIENT NAHUA (AZTEC) POETRY

Introduction 3
The Flower Songs of Hungry Coyote 15
The Life of Hungry Coyote 45

THE SONGS OF DZITBALCHE   55
ANCIENT MAYAN POETRY

Introduction 57
The Songs of Dzitbalche 63
The Life of Ah Bam 103

THE SACRED HYMNS OF PACHACUTI   109
ANCIENT INCA POETRY

Introduction 111
The Sacred Hymns of Pachacuti 125
The Life of Pachacuti Inca Yupanqui 149

Selected Bibliography 157

v

Preface

The idea of ancient American poets and poetry may sound strange to some ears. In the United States we are usually taught that American poetry is an extension of English poetry, in Canada French poetry is often included, and in Latin America schools teach the Spanish and Portuguese traditions. Yet there were rich traditions of poetry on this continent long before the first European colonists arrived.

The ancient Mayas and Nahuas recorded their literature, culture, and history using indigenous writing systems, and the Incas recorded theirs on knotted strings called quipus. The Maya and Nahua screenfold books and the Inca quipus were almost all destroyed in the first years of the Conquest. When these old recording systems were forbidden by the conquerors, many people in each of these cultures quickly learned to write their own languages in the European alphabet and used it to record their own cultures for their own uses. Much of the oldest American literature has come down to us from these early Native books and manuscripts, written in alphabetic Nahuatl (Aztec), Maya, and Quechua (Inca). Among the literature they contain is a body of poetry by ancient Amerindians in the original languages and biographies of some of the poets.

The Flower Songs of Nezahualcoyotl (Nahua-Aztec), the Songs of Dzitbalche (Yucatec Maya), and the Sacred Hymns of Pachacuti (Inca) are all roughly contemporary in their dates of composition, around 1440, though the manuscripts containing them were written over a century later.

Most of these poems were meant to be accompanied by music, which makes them "lyric" poetry in the original sense of the word. Pachacuti's hymns were sung. Hungry Coyote's flower songs were recited over a drum cadence. Some of the Dzitbalche "dances" were surely sung, while others appear to have been spoken. Whether they are poems or songs or both is ultimately a hollow question, since no true line exists between poetry and song.

By the same token, no true line exists between oral and written literature. The very fact that language is based on words means that it cannot stray too far from the oral and must return to it. While the Mayas were the only Amerindian group to develop a complete writing system to record their literature, most pre-Conquest cultures had highly sophisticated mnemonic aids and traditions of memorization. The Nahuas used pictographs and ideographs; the Incas used the complex knots of the quipu. Many of the northern Amerindians likewise used symbols to record their history and culture, such as the Lenape's Walam Olum, both pictographic Algonquin chronicle and historical epic poetry. Melody, meter, and rhyme are of course universal mnemonic devices for poetry and song. The embedding of poems and songs into ceremonies also served to preserve them intact.

We know much about the lives of these poets because they were also prominent leaders, and Amerindian historians recorded detailed chronicles and biographies of their leading families. The civilizations of the Nahuas, Mayas, and Incas were all aristocratic. Nezahualcoyotl and Pachacuti were both kings during cultural peaks of their civilizations, so we know copious details about their lives. We have less information about Ah Bam, who was a member of the lower nobility and wrote during the colonial period, although many of his songs are ancient. Commoners as well as aristocrats were poets in these cultures, and early Amerindian manuscripts record many of their wonderful poems and songs, but these remain anonymous.

The sophisticated and cultured world that produced these indigenous poets was disrupted and destroyed by conquest. The European invasion included a campaign by the conquerors to blot out all memory of the accomplishments of the native cultures. Their children were educated to believe that the colonizers saved them by destroying the old culture. It is only in recent times, as the descendants of both colonized and colonizers struggle to heal our cultures today, that the world is ripe to appreciate the accomplishments of the native civilizations.

A large body of ancient and early indigenous literature has emerged, and more continues to appear.

Nahuatl, Maya, and Quechua are all still living languages, widely spoken today. They remain the three largest Amerindian language groups. Contemporary Nahuatl, Maya, and Quechua have of course changed considerably from the languages in these poems, just as English has changed from the language of Chaucer or Shakespeare. Of the twenty million people who currently speak a Native American language, about sixty percent speak one of these three. Nahuatl speakers today total over one million and are spread across central Mexico. The Mayan languages together total about four million speakers in southern Mexico, Yucatan, and Central America, with about a half million speaking Yucatec Maya. Quechua has seven million speakers, mostly in Peru, Bolivia, and Ecuador.

The apparent divide between Anglo America and Latin America conforms to the boundaries of colonialism, not of native culture. There has always been a cultural continuity between the northern and southern Amerindian nations. The resurgence of Amerindian consciousness and nationalism today, both north and south, makes this clear. These poets and poems are really part of our pan-American cultural heritage, our American roots. That is why it is important for us today to reclaim, as much as possible, knowledge of the world that was destroyed. The inheritors of colonialism owe much to the descendants of the colonized. Recognition of their classic literature is long overdue.

The only classical Amerindian work sometimes embraced in the canon of world literature is the *Popol Vuh* (*Pop Wuj*) of the Quiche Maya. On rare occasions the *Books of Chilam Balam* and the *Apu Ollantay* are included. Yet there are many other works that deserve to be widely read. The Flower Songs of Nezahualcoyotl, the Songs of Dzitbalche, and the Sacred Hymns of Pachacuti are the patrimony of us all and deserve to take their places as classics of American literature.

The poems and poets of this amazing lost American world are of immense importance to our common future.

About These Translations

I began these translations two decades ago after a conversation with the great translator-poet Jack Hirschman. I had been reading ancient indigenous literature unavailable in English and thought it contained knowledge that could change the world if it could be brought to light. He encouraged me to try to change the world.

To do these translations, I collected all the available original texts and previous translations (mostly in Spanish), as well as various dictionaries and grammars of the original languages. I immersed myself in the languages one at a time—Nahuatl, Yucatec Maya, and Quechua—using previous translations as gateways into the original texts.

These translations are literary interpretations designed to communicate the original meanings and beauty, as opposed to being literal scholarly translations. My approach is to try to dig down to the original intent and meaning and bring those out in the translation. A too-literal approach winds up focusing on the trees and missing the forest.

I have followed the lead of previous translators in cutting up the lines and modifying the word division and punctuation in the original language to fit the particular translation. Although this may be at variance with the original manuscript, it makes the poetry much more accessible and easier to follow in the original language. The layouts reflect the interpretations inherent in the translations.

Indigenous words used in the commentaries are in modern spelling, except for traditional spellings of names and words adopted into the English language. The texts are in their colonial orthography. In Spanish-language texts, accents in conformity with Spanish grammatical rules are customarily inserted into Amerindian words, the bulk of which are names of people and places, such as Dzitbalché, Nezahualcóyotl, Manco Cápac. In modern English, some books follow the Spanish usage, while others do not. Here we will follow Amerindian usage, so those names will be spelled without the accents: Dzitbalche, Nezahualcoyotl, and Manco Capac.

I hope these translations reflect some of the brilliant light of the original poems.

The Flower Songs of Nezahualcoyotl

Ancient Nahua (Aztec) Poetry

Nezahualcoyotl. Codex Ixtlilxochitl.

INTRODUCTION

THE FLOWER SONGS OF HUNGRY COYOTE

THE LIFE OF HUNGRY COYOTE

INTRODUCTION

Nezahualcoyotl (Hungry Coyote) was considered by his peers to be the greatest poet of ancient Mexico. His compositions had vast influence, stylistically and in content. Filled with thought, symbol, and myth, his poetry moved his people's culture so deeply that after his death generations of poets to follow would stand by the *huehuetl* drum and cry, "I am Nezahualcoyotl, I am Hungry Coyote," and sing his poems and keep them alive.

Nezahualcoyotl was not only a great lyric poet, but was famed as an architect, engineer, city planner, reluctant warrior, lawgiver, and philosopher. The cultural institutions he established included a library of hieroglyphic books, a zoological garden-arboretum, and a self-governing academy of scholars and poets. He led his city-state out of foreign domination and transformed it into a wellspring of art and culture. As the seventh ruler *(tlacatecuhtli)* of Texcoco, a large city on the north shore of Lake Texcoco, ten miles across the water from the capital of the Aztecs, Hungry Coyote promoted a renewal of Toltec learning based on the peaceful religion of Quetzalcoatl at the very moment when the Aztec cult of sacrifice was coming into ascendancy. All the Nahuatl-speaking city-states in the Valley of Mexico looked to Hungry Coyote's Texcoco as the cultural center of their world.

The story is not a simple one and the chronicles of his life themselves are contradictory. However, the spirit of paradox is embedded in the soul of ancient Mexico.

The complex surfaces of many flower songs (*xochicuicame*) often make them difficult to understand for many people in our culture. We do not have ready categories for them and they require effort. Yet they contain many gems of universal lasting value and offer great rewards to those willing to make that effort.

NAHUA POETS, POETRY, AND CEREMONIAL FLOWERS

Most of the flower songs that have come down to us are in two collections from the second half of the sixteenth century. Although transcribed as they were sung at that time, they clearly contain many songs and parts of songs that are much older.

The form of the flower song as it has come down to us seems to have had its beginning in the generation before Hungry Coyote. But it was his generation, and particularly he himself, who perfected the form and brought it to its greatest heights.

Hungry Coyote lived at a moment when the anonymous singer, *cuicani*, of his people's tradition, who received verses in a song quest, began to speak of personal feelings and ideas and emerged a remembered poet. In form and content Hungry Coyote was an innovator: he perfected a style that numerous other poets copied. He was also part of a poetic movement, a generation of poets and singers who were moving beyond the earlier modes of Nahua poetry.

From the older tradition come the anonymous sacred hymns, twenty of which have come down to us transcribed by Bernardino de Sahagún. While most of the sacred hymns are direct and formal, the flower songs can take off wildly in many directions from a theme. Flower songs were a channel to invoke the deity in an individual and personal way. They were also connected with the ingestion of hallucinatory mushrooms and similar substances. Poetry and art were ecstatic gifts of the gods.

Flower songs kept close to the rhythms and patterns of speech. Their poetics included the repetition of ideas in couplets or parallel form, a tendency to speak in metaphors, and the use of repeating synonyms and metonyms. Kennings were frequent, two words used together becoming a traditional metaphorical name for a third thing, such as "eagles and jaguars" meaning "warriors"; "mat and chair" meaning "authority"; or "flower and song" meaning "poetry."

The texts indicate no regular length of line or stanza, no rhyme or meter. The variety seems almost Whitmanesque. Refrains appear, change, and disappear in no strict pattern or order. Many of the poems as we have them seem long and confusing. Many seem to break into different voices in different stanzas, often in dialog, but not always. Repetitive syllables such as "Ohuaya, Ohuaya" follow verses of many of the songs. These are vocables or litanies, which have no translatable meaning but define the stanza.

Flower songs were performed to the open-hand beat of the *huehuetl* drum, each poem to a distinct cadence, the beat patterns preserved along with the poems in some of the ancient texts.

The themes of flower songs seem limited, yet they were put together in endless variations: meditations on the meaning of life and death, on the pleasures of living and loving, on friendship, on relations between the poet and the deity; lamentations on the brevity of life and fame; elegies on poetry; memorials to great leaders; celebrations of cities and the people; or verses on the ecstasies of singing and war. They were sometimes composed for a particular occasion to make a critical commentary on it.

The two prophetic poems of Nezahualcoyotl that we have only in translation by Ixtlilxochitl do not seem to be in quite the same style as the songs in the two major collections. The style is more straightforward and grammatical. However, the originals may have been more similar.

Although these poems are usually all known as "flower songs" today, to Hungry Coyote and his contemporaries, the word *xochicuicatl*, "flower song," described only one particular style among many that we usually include in the genre. *Xochicuicame* were literally songs about flowers or relating to the ceremonies of the goddess Xochiquetzal. This entire body of poetry/song became known as "flower songs" because the word "flower" and its cognates occur in them so often, not only when they are referring to flowers per se, but as symbols, metaphors, and imagery with many different implications. The Nahuatl phrase "*in xochitl in cuicatl*" meant "flower and song" literally, but figuratively meant "poetry" or "art."

There were two general categories of song and dance, *netotiliztin* and *macehualiztin*. The *netotiliztin*, "dances of joy," were the worldly dances associated with entertainment. They were performed during the fiesta parts of holidays as well as in other venues. Though they might refer to religious ceremonies, they were not a ritual part of them.

The *macehualiztin*, dances of merit, were the sacred hymns, a ritual part of religious ceremonies. The flower songs of Hungry Coyote were *netotiliztin*, "dances of joy."

There were many modes of *netotiliztin*. *Xochicuicame* (flower songs proper) and *xopancuicame* (spring songs) were spiritual and lyric. *Yaocuicame* or *cuauhtlicuicame* (warrior songs) were about heroes and hunters. *Icnoccuicame* or *tlaocolhcuicame* (orphan and suffering songs) lamented life's insecurities. Besides these were *huehuecuicame* (songs of old people), *cihuacuicame* (songs of women), and others. There were also various regional styles: Texcocan, Mexican, Otomi, Tepanecan, Acolhuan, Tlaxcalan, Huastec, and Totonac. Otomi style songs were not in Nahuatl but in the Chichimec language. Hungry Coyote wrote flower songs in Otomi as well as in Nahuatl.

Hungry Coyote's flower songs are the earliest ones that we can attribute to a known poet, except for one song by Tlaltecatzin, a poet of his father's generation. Tlaltecatzin's poem is a curious one in that it combines sex and death, while overt erotic elements and love themes are missing in all other flower songs that have come down to us. Yet there is something incoherently ecstatic in the flower songs. Moreover, there are reports that Nahua love songs were actually common. It is perhaps from this combination of the profanely secular with the sacred, from this duality, that the form of flower songs originally sprang.

While the sacred hymns were sung in and around the temples, the flower songs were performed more often in homes and in other secular venues, as well as in the house of song, the music school established as an adjunct to a temple in every Nahua city.

Poet-singers, called *cuicapicque* (songmakers) or *xochitlahtoane* (flowerspeakers), performed publicly on the many holidays and at the festivals and religious ceremonies that filled the year in the Nahua world. They also presented their works in circles of poets and musicians, which met regularly. Both nobles and commoners, women as well as men, could be song-makers. Many of the *cuicapicque* were professionals. All the noble houses had their singers who composed chants about their own glorious deeds and those of their ancestors. The religious sects also kept salaried composers who lived in the temples and created divine chants praising the gods. Besides singing their own original compositions, *cuicapicque* would perform and embroider great works by other poets. However, many of the songmakers who composed flower songs, like Hungry Coyote, were not salaried professionals. Many men who did not have the temperament of a warrior found this as a road to personal achievement and success. These independent singers received their primary payment in praise, but were also often rewarded with valuable gifts from the king or nobles for their work.

Sometimes a group of poets would perform together, each poet taking a turn with a poem on the same theme and creating a dialog. On occasion they spoke through the voices of historic or mythologic personages. The poetic dialog that resulted, the "dialog of the songs," approached theater or drama.

The poets would usually perform accompanied by a *huehuetl* drum, *teponaztli*, and sometimes a flute. The *huehuetl* was an upright drum crafted from a hollowed log two to four feet high with a diameter of twelve to eighteen inches, open at the bottom, standing on three legs cut from its base, with skin stretched across the top. It was usually carved with designs and symbols and was beaten with the hands. The *teponaztli* was a horizontal wooden drum or "gong," hollowed in the center but left closed on both ends, flattened on top, with two tongues of different lengths cut into it. The *teponaztli* was beaten with rubber-tipped sticks. Nahua musicians also played flutes, double flutes, triple flutes, and pan pipes, using a pentatonic or five-note scale. These instruments were all six to eight inches long, usually of clay, but sometimes also of bamboo or bone.

Singing and music were part of everyone's education. In the evening after school at the *telpochcalli*, the school for the common people, both girls and boys went to the *cuicacalli*, the house of song, which stood next to one of the temples. In the Toltec conception, a city did not really exist until it had established a place for the drums, that is, a house of song. This was a singing, music and dance school, as well as a residence for the teachers, and consisted of many large rooms around a courtyard. Attendance was required of all boys and girls, who were taught separately but brought together in the courtyard for common dances. In the house of song were lodged the *huehuetl, teponaztli*, rattles, flutes, shell trumpets, costumes, and regalia of the dancers. Taught at these schools were primarily the sacred hymns and the dances that went with them.

During the day, before the girls and boys arrived for their studies, the house of song doubled as a dance hall for warriors and *ahuilnenque*, "pleasure women." As Friar Diego Durán, who grew up in Texcoco, describes it around the year 1570:

> Let us now speak of the ordinary dance which the warriors and soldiers performed daily, during the daytime, in that same building and school of dance. They went there to dance as a pastime . . . These warriors, known as *tequihuaque*, went there and, dressed in their best, danced in fine style. When one of these men saw a harlot [sic] looking at him with a certain amount of interest, he beckoned to her and, taking her by the hand, danced with her in that dance. Thus he spent the entire [day until] evening with that woman, holding her by the hand while they danced . . . (*Book of the Gods*, 298).

He describes the rhythms as lively. "These were dances and songs of pleasure, known as 'dances of youth,' during which they sang songs of love and flirtation . . ." (ibid., 295).

In contrast, Durán wrote that the sacred hymns "were sung slowly and seriously; these were sung and danced by the lords on solemn and important occasions, and were intoned, some with moderation and calm" (ibid.). The sacred hymns were sung or chanted both inside and outside the temples, addressed directly to specific deities. A number of sacred hymns have come down to us, twenty of them preserved by Padre Bernardino de Sahagún around 1558 to 1560 in the Florentine codex. None has any attribution of authorship. Sahagún wrote of them, "The children who went to the *calmecac* learned by memory all the verses of songs to sing, called divine songs, whose verses were written in their books in characters." The *calmecac* was a special school for children of the nobility and gifted children and prepared them to become leaders and priests. Each *calmecac* was located adjacent to a temple and closely connected with it. Instruction there was more extensive than in the *telpochcaltin*, the schools for the common people run by the clans, where the children were taught a standard curriculum and then brought over to the house of song at the temple in the evening for musical and ritual instruction.

Groups of poets and elders called *tlapizcatzitzin* (conservators) approved new compositions and taught divine songs in honor of gods. They called public meetings to teach the songs to all the people. They were still singing and dancing *macehualiztin* after the

Conquest, for Durán witnessed them. "These songs were so sad that just the rhythm and dance saddens one. I have seen these danced occasionally with religious chants, and they were so sad that I was filled with melancholy and woe" (300).

He goes on to say that, although he was fluent in Nahuatl, he really did not understand the words to the songs.

> All the native lays are interwoven with such obscure metaphors that there is hardly a man who can understand them unless they are studied in a very special way and explained so as to penetrate their meaning. For this reason I have intentionally set myself to listen with much attention to what is sung; and while the words and the terms of the metaphors seem nonsense to me, afterwards, having discussed and conferred, they seem to be admirable sentences, both in the divine things composed today and in the worldly songs. (299-300)

The soil in which flower songs grew was a combination of the profane and the sacred, the social and the ceremonial.

The flower songs that we have are not about love and flirtation, like the "dances of youth." They are poems of a high seriousness, but sung to the same lively rhythms as other worldly songs. The transcribers simply might have not written down the more bawdy songs.

The friar goes on, describing the custom:

> The dance they most enjoyed was the one in which they crowned and adorned themselves with flowers. A house of flowers was erected on the main pyramid.... They also erected artificial trees covered with fragrant flowers where they seated the goddess Xochiquetzalli. During the dance some boys dressed as birds and others as butterflies descended. They were richly decked with fine green, blue, red, and yellow feathers. These youths ascended the trees, climbing from limb to limb, sucking the dew of the flowers. Then the "gods" appeared, each wearing robes such as the idols wore on the altars—a man or a woman dressed in the guise of each. With their blowguns in their hands they went around shooting at the "birds" who were in the trees. Then the Goddess of Flowers—Xochiquetzalli—came out to receive them, took them by the hand, making them sit next to her, treating them with great honor and respect, as such divinities deserved. There she presented them with flowers and gave them to smoke, and then she made her representatives come to amuse them. This was the most solemn dance in the land, and I rarely see another one danced today unless it is by exception.... (296)

Now we are clearly in the realm of the *xochicuicatl*, the flower song. We have four songs that Hungry Coyote composed for the Farewell to the Flowers or for a similar festival held in the spring: "Stand Up, Beat Your Drum," "Song of Spring," "Already It Begins," and "The Flower Tree."

> Among the most solemn feasts was the one called Farewell to the Flowers, which meant that frost was coming and flowers would wither and dry up. A solemn festivity, filled with rejoicing and merrymaking, was held to bid them farewell. On that same day they commemorated a goddess named Xochiquetzalli, which means "Flowery Plumage."
>
> On this day they were as happy as could be, the same happiness and delight they feel today on smelling any kind of flower, whether it have an agreeable or a displeasing scent, as long as it is a flower. They become the happiest people in the world smelling them, for these natives in general are most sensuous and pleasure-loving. They find gladness and joy in spending the entire day smelling a little flower or a bouquet made

of different kinds of flowers; their gifts are accompanied by them; they relieve the tediousness of journeys with flowers. To sum up, they find the smelling of flowers so comforting that they even stave off and manage to survive hunger by smelling them. Thus they passed their lives among flowers in such blindness and darkness, since they had been deceived and persuaded by the devil, who had observed their love for blossoms and flowers. . . .

On this day their persons, temples, houses and streets were adorned with flowers. . . . Thus decorated with flowers, they engaged in different dances, merrymaking, festivities, and farces, all filled with gladness and good cheer. All this was in honor of and reverence for flowers. This day was called Xochilhuitl, which means "Feast of the Flowers," and no other finery—gold, silver, stones, feathers—was worn on this day—only flowers. Besides being the day of the flowers it was the day of a goddess, who, as I have said, was called Xochiquetzal. This goddess was the patroness of painters, embroiderers, weavers, silversmiths, sculptors, and all those whose profession it was to imitate nature in crafts and in drawing. All held this goddess to be their patroness, and her feast was specially solemnized by them. . . . (238)

The Feast of the Flowers was continued after the Conquest in a changed form, like so much of the old religion. The last day of the twenty-day Farewell to the Flowers was October 26, only a few days before the Days of the Dead, still celebrated today in Mexican communities with the same flowers, marigolds.

THE GIVER OF LIFE: THE TOLTEC DUALITY OF QUETZALCOATL

Hungry Coyote addressed many songs to the deity without ever mentioning a proper name. Instead, he (and the other Nahua poets) called Him by certain of His aspects or qualities such as Life Giver, One for Whom All Live, He Who Makes the World Live, Author of Life, Highest Arbiter, Lord of the Far and Near, Lord of the With and the By, or Inventor of Himself. These were all epithets for Tloque Nahuaque, the Unknown God, who was also the Creator, Quetzalcoatl, the "white" Tezcatlipoca.

From the time of the Toltecs, the Valley of Mexico was dominated by the clash of forces represented by the deities Quetzalcoatl and the "black" Tezcatlipoca.

Quetzalcoatl was the Feathered (or Plumed) Serpent who lives in the wind, the deity of civilization, of culture, knowledge, peace, fertility, the bringer of the arts and crafts, writing, singing, and poetry. He gave life to the first people of this fifth world and the gift of corn for sustenance. Quetzalcoatl was closely associated with Ehecatl, deity of the wind, and Tlaloc, master of rain. Tlaloc in turn was associated with Coatlicue, goddess of the earth. Quetzalcoatl had been the patron deity of the great city-state Teotihuacan, predecessor to the Toltecs.

Tezcatlipoca, "Smoking Mirror," the night sky, was the deity of destruction and death, the patron of warriors and sorcerers. Tezcatlipoca was closely associated with Mixcoatl, the old Chichimec deity of the hunt, and later with Huitzilopochtli, patron of the Aztec warrior orders. Tezcatlipoca, unlike Quetzalcoatl, demanded human sacrifice. This dichotomy played out in history as it did in myth.

In the late tenth century, under the Toltec chieftain-priest Quetzalcoatl-Topiltzin, follower of the Plumed Serpent, the city of Tula (Tollan) became a great center of a cultural renaissance in which all the arts and sciences blossomed. It was the inheritor of the earlier culture of Teotihuacan and predecessor to Hungry Coyote's Texcoco. This cultural renaissance was destined to be short-lived.

There were two distinct groups among the Toltecs of Tula: the Nonoalcas, who were blood descendants of Teotihuacan and followers of Quetzalcoatl, and the Tolteca-Chichimecas, who were the newly acculturated groups, wanderers from the north only recently come into contact with civilization, followers of Tezcatlipoca.

According to the legendary history as described by Nezahualcoyotl's descendant Ixtlilxochitl and other early chroniclers, a struggle developed between the chieftain Quetzalcoatl-Topiltzin and Tezcatlipoca-Huemac, the high priest of the Toltec warrior orders. Quetzalcoatl-Topiltzin was a Nonoalca and Tezcatlipoca-Huemac was a Tolteca-Chichimeca.

Quetzalcoatl-Topiltzin tried to lead the people of Tula to reject the deities of militarism and sacrifice and instead pay peaceful homage to the Feathered Serpent. But Tezcatlipoca-Huemac grew jealous and demanded human sacrifice. A mortal struggle ensued.

Rejecting civil war, Quetzalcoatl-Topiltzin yielded the city to Tezcatlipoca-Huemac, leading his followers out of Tula, disappearing into exile toward the east, toward Tlillan Tlapallan, "land of the red and black," where according to the legend, he became the morning star, the planet Venus, and from where he would return someday to reclaim his throne. According to another version, he led his followers to Yucatan and built Chichen-Itza.

Without Quetzalcoatl-Topiltzin the city of Tula lost its cohesion, spirit, and will. When attacked by new waves of Chichimec bands, it succumbed. Tezcatlipoca-Huemac met with a violent death. Bands of Toltec refugees scattered to the shores of Lake Texcoco and many other places in the Valley of Mexico, farther south to the land of the Mixtecas and beyond. Tula in its heyday was soon looked back on as a golden age.

When Xolotl and his Chichimec band established control over the region, Xolotl took a Toltec princess as his wife. By mixing his family with Toltec descendants, Xolotl's lineage became Toltec. The ruling lineages of every province and city in the valley of Mexico soon all vied to connect their family lines with those of the Toltecs. This connection became an essential credential to power. With the blood connection came the infusion of Toltec culture and values.

But the dominant Toltec culture that the Valley of Mexico inherited was the legacy of Tezcatlipoca, not Quetzalcoatl. When a new ruler was sworn in, it was to Tezcatlipoca that he took his oath of faith, and from whom he asked guidance. The Feathered Serpent's cult continued in a lesser capacity, often in disguise, as "the white Tezcatlipoca."

So it was in the time of Hungry Coyote. That is why the name of Quetzalcoatl never appears in any of his songs, yet underlies every verse.

However, according to Toltec cosmology, all divinity proceeds from Omeyocan, "The Place of Duality." So while Quetzalcoatl and Tezcatlipoca were antagonists, opposites, light and dark, they were also associated with each other; they were part of each other.

Before this world there were four previous worlds created and destroyed, according to the myth, and Quetzalcoatl and Tezcatlipoca took turns as creator and destroyer.

Tezcatlipoca had four aspects, which corresponded to the four directions and also to different deities. The "black" aspect was the original Tezcatlipoca, the night sky; the "red" Tezcatlipoca was Xipe Totec, god of spring; the "blue" Tezcatlipoca was Huitzilopochtli, tribal god of the Aztecs, deity of the sun; and the "white" Tezcatlipoca was Quetzalcoatl. Thus Tezcatlipoca was both destroyer and creator.

A Lexicon of Flowers

To understand the concept and function of flower songs, we need to look more deeply at the special meanings that flowers had for the Nahua people in Hungry Coyote's time.

Xochiquetzal (Flower Quetzal), goddess of flowers and love, was the first wife of Tlaloc, deity of rain. It should be no surprise that flowers were associated with life-giving water, particularly in a place where the sun could be brutal. Xochiquetzal, however, was kidnapped by Tezcatlipoca and made his wife. (Tlaloc got over it and found another wife.) She was also associated with a male counterpart, Xochipilli, "prince of flowers," deity of summer, patron of love, dance, and games. He was sometimes associated with the "red" Tezcatlipoca. Xochiquetzal and Xochipilli were the patrons of the "floating gardens" of Xochimilco at the east end of Lake Texcoco.

Xochiquetzal was also connected with Xochitl (Flower), one of the twenty calendric day signs, the twentieth sign, the last day of every month. Xochitl was associated with masters and craftsmen. Xochitl people, according to the astrology, tended to be clean, diligent, hard-working, and to make a living with the skill of their hands. Men born under it were likely to be workers in "crafts that imitate nature" such as painters, metalworkers, weavers, sculptors, or carvers. Women born under it were likely to be weavers, embroiderers, fine home decorators, well-adorned dressers, and skilled at decorative presentation as cooks.

Poems or songs were "necklaces of flowers." Poetry was also "the floral drum." The beauty of a song was "upright flowers." The places where poets and singers met were the "houses of the flowers," "arbors of the precious flowers," "flowery patios," or "mats of flowers."

The Nahuas had four after-death lands, three of them lush garden paradises: Tamoanchan, the western "flower land" for women who died in childbirth; Tlalocan, the tropical "place of the flowering tree" for those who died by water; and Tonatiuhichan, the florid garden of dawn for those who died in battle. Mictlan, the fourth after-death land, was flowerless, shadowy, and chill, located in the north; there the dead who had not earned a place in one of the paradises underwent a series of trials leading to final peace and dissolution.

The word "flower" was also redolent with associations of war and sacrifice. "Flowery death" meant death in war. The "flowers" were the warriors whose lives were so brief and precarious, the captives, the sacrificial victims. Prisoners were "flowers of the battle," "precious flowers of the jaguar," "flowers of war," "flowers of the eagle," or "flowers of the shield." Battles were "flowers of the heart of the plain," "fragrant flowers of the jaguars," or "flowers of battle." To say that "the flowers of war intoxicate me," meant "the fervor of war excites me." "Paper flowers" were insignia worn by the gods and by sacrificial victims. The human heart was spoken of as the "flower of God," or "flower of the heart."

Authorship and Transmission

The vast majority of the Nahua songwriters were anonymous, but about forty Nahua poets have been identified (primarily by Garibay and León-Portilla), most of them nobles. Hungry Coyote is the author of some thirty-six to forty-one songs (depending on how one counts), the most by far of any Nahua poet. Tecayehuatzin is the author of nine, Ayocuan three. We have two songs, or fragments, by at least sixteen other poets.

The poems that were written down in Spanish script in the sixteenth century are transcriptions of songs as they were sung and chanted at that time. The singers of that era quoted earlier poets—the great classic poets of the culture—in their poems, often incorporating, developing, and expanding the earlier songs. Much of the poetry of Nezahualcoyotl has come down to us as quoted fragments and lyrics embedded into the songs of these later poets and singers. Nezahualcoyotl appears as a speaker in various dialog poems.

Many of the attributions of authorship are by internal evidence. The scholar A. M. Garibay was the first to interpret the "I am" formula as an indigenous Mexican convention indicating signature or authorship. In the example of Hungry Coyote, his interpretation is based on the word "niNezahualcoyotl," which occurs frequently and means literally, "I Hungry Coyote." According to this interpretation, in the context of the poem it means "This is a poem by Hungry Coyote" or "I am performing a poem of Hungry Coyote's." It might also mean, "I am performing a poem inspired by, or in the style of, Hungry Coyote." It could also indicate that the singer is calling down Hungry Coyote's spirit. The texts as we have them do not always make this clear, so there is much room for debate over what is and what is not a poem by Hungry Coyote, or where one begins and ends.

Just the mention of Hungry Coyote's name in a poem obviously does not make it his. There are also poems addressed to Hungry Coyote by other poets, and poems about Hungry Coyote. The scholar John Bierhorst denies the interpretation of signature entirely and does not accept the attribution of any classical Nahuatl poems to any particular poet; he sees the "I am" formula as meaning that the singer is calling down a spirit.

While modern scholars may dispute the attribution to Hungry Coyote of any particular poem, it is clear that the ancient Nahuas themselves considered Hungry Coyote to be their greatest classical composer of songs, and that the later Nahua poets thought they were singing his songs or singing in his style. The acceptance of these songs as representative of at least the spirit of Hungry Coyote's work brings us as close to the truth as the mists of time will permit.

I have tried to include a representative selection of the flower songs in this collection.

Drum Accompaniment And Vocables

The poems were originally performed accompanied by the large two-tone *huehuetl* drum. The beat patterns for a number of poems are preserved in the texts.

       Code: to = low tone stressed
               ti = high tone stressed
               co = low tone unstressed
               qui = high tone unstressed

For example, below are the cadences and codas for the five sections of "Song of Hungry Coyote," *Cantares Mexicanos* #46.

Section # 1:   Totoco totoco tico totoco totoco.
At the end: tico titico titico tico.

Section # 2:   Quititi quititi quiti quiti.
At the end: tocoto tocoti tocototocoti.

Section # 3:   Tico toco tocoto.
At the end: ticoto ticoto.

Section # 4:   Toto tiquiti tiquiti.
At the end: tocotico tocoti tototitiqui tototitiquiti.

Section # 5:   Toco toco tiqui tiqui.
At the end: tocotico tocoti.

In many of the songs, each stanza ends with repeated vocables, syllables without meaning outside of the rhythm of the song. They give structure to songs where lines and stanzas have widely varying lengths. Vocables will be indicated by italics.

The Nahuatl Language

Nahuatl was the language of those Mesoamericans commonly known today as "Aztecs." However, the word "Aztec" properly refers to only the inhabitants of the city-state Tenochtitlan, while Nahuatl was the *lingua franca* of the entire Valley of Mexico, comprising many city-states, stemming back to the fabled Toltec city Tula and probably to Teotihuacan.

Today Nahuatl-speaking people are still one of Mexico's largest indigenous groups, numbering over one million spread over the central parts of the country. Nahuatl-speaking people are also now commonly referred to by researchers as "Nahuas."

Many dialects of modern Nahuatl are quite different from the language of Hungry Coyote, although some are surprisingly similar. The shape of the modern language was of course strongly influenced by centuries of proximity to Spanish.

The language of these poems is far more complex than conversational Nahuatl. It is considered an esoteric language.

Word order is very flexible in Nahuatl. Secondary elements in a sentence often have only a loose connection with the core, through proximity rather than through syntax. That results in Nahuatl's having an expansive ambiguity and evocativeness, rather than the linear logic we are accustomed to in English.

Nahuatl creates long sentence-words by joining two or more roots of verbs and/or nouns, then affixing particles to provide other information. Thus subject, verb, and object all become part of the same sentence-word.

SIMPLIFIED GUIDE TO NAHUATL PRONUNCIATION*

Vowels as in Spanish

Consonants as in English, except:
- x = /sh/
- z = /s/
- qu before e or i = /k/
- qu, cu, uc before a or o = /kw/
- h is a glottal stop
- tl is voiceless, with the same point of articulation as for /t/, but with air released at the sides
- tz = /ts/
- ll = /l/, not as ll in Spanish
- uh, hu = /w/

Stress on the penultimate syllable.

LINGUISTIC GUIDE TO NAHUATL PRONUNCIATION

	phoneme	alphabetic representation
vowels	/a/, /ā/	a
	/e/, /ē/	e
	/i/, /ī/	i, y, j
	/o/, /ō/	o, u
consonants	/p/	p
	/t/	t
	/k/	c, qu
	/ʔ/	h *(usually not written)*
	/tˢ/	tz
	/tˡ/	tl
	/ch/	ch
	/kʷ/	cu, uc, qu
	/s/	c, ç, s, z
	/sh/	x
	/m/	m, n
	/n/	n
	/l/	l
	/w/	uh, hu, u, v, o
	/y/	y, i, j

* This pronunciation guide and all that follow utilize the systems of linguistic notation found in *Merriam-Webster's Collegiate Dictionary*, 11th edition. For sounds not included therein, we have used the International Phonetic Alphabet.

INTRODUCTION/THE FLOWER SONGS

The Flower Songs of Hungry Coyote

Nezahualcoyotl sees a vision. Codex Xolotl.

(1)

IN CHOLOLIZTLI CUICATL

O nen notlacatl. Ayahue!

O nen nonquizaco teotl ichan in tlalticpac. Ninotolinia. Ohuaya ohuaya!

In ma on nel nonquiz in ma on nel nontlacat ah niquitohua yece. Yeehuaya! Tlen naiz anonohuaco tepilhuan? At teixco ninemi? Quen huel xon mimati. Aya Ohuaya ohuaya!

Ye ya nonehuaz in tlalticpac? Ye ya tle in nolhuil? Zan nitoliniya tonehua noyollo tinocniuh in ayaxcan in tlalticpac ye nican. Ohuaya ohuaya.

Quen in nemohua—Aya!—in tenahuac? Mach ilihuiztia nemia tehuic teyaconi. Aya! Nemi zan ihuiyan zan icemelia. In zan nonopechteca zan nitolotinemi a in tenahuac. Ohuaya ohuaya.

Zan ye ica nichoca—Yeehuaya!—nicnotlamati no nicnocahualoc in tenahuac tlalticpac. Quen quinequi noyollo—Yeehuaya!—ipal nemohuani? Ma oc melel on quiza a icnopillotl. Huiya! Ma oc timalihui—Aya!—monahuac titeotl. At ya nech miquitlani? Ohuaya ohuaya.

Azomo ye nelli tipaqui ti ya nemi tlalticpac? Ah ca za tinemi ihuan ti hual paqui in tlalticpac. Ah ca mochi ihui titotolinia. Ah ca no chichic teopouhqui tenahuac ye nican. Ohuaya ohuaya.

Ma xi icnotlamati noyollo. Yeehuaya! Maca oc tle xic yococa. Yeehuaya! Ye nelli in ayaxcan nicnopiltihua in tlalticpac. Ye nelli cococ ye otimalihuico in motloc monahuac in ipal nemohua. Yyao yyahue ahuayye oo Huiya.

Zan niquintemohua—Aya!—niquilnamiqui in tocnihuan. Cuix oc ceppa huitze in cuix oc nemiquihui? Zan cen ti ya polihuia zan cen ye nican in tlalticpac. Maca cocoya inyollo itloc inahuac in ipal nemohua. Yyao yyahue ahuayye oo Huiya.

ROMANCES DE LOS SEÑORES #36 (21R-22V)

(De Nezahualcoyotzin cuando andaba huyendo del rey de Azcapotzalco.)

(1)

SONG OF THE FLIGHT

In vain I was born. *Ayahue.*

In vain I left the house of God and came to earth. I am so wretched! *Ohuaya, ohuaya.*

I wish I'd never been born, truly that I'd never come to earth. That's what I say. But what is there to do? Do I have to live among the people? What then? Princes, tell me! *Aya. Ohuaya ohuaya.*

Do I have to stand on earth? What is my destiny? My heart suffers. I am unfortunate. You were hardly my friend here on earth, Life Giver. *Ohuaya ohuaya.*

How to live—*Aya*—among the people? Does he who sustains and lifts men have no discretion? Go, friends, live in peace, pass your life in calm! While I have to live stooped, with my head bent down when I am among the people. *Ohuaya ohuaya.*

For this I cry—*Yeehuya!*—feeling desolate, abandoned among men on the earth. How do you decide your heart—*Yeehuya!*—Life Giver? Already your anger is vanishing, your compassion welling! *Aya!* I am at your side, God. Do you plan my death? *Ohuaya ohuaya.*

Is it true we take pleasure, we who live on earth? Is it certain that we live to enjoy ourselves on earth? But we are all so filled with grief. Are bitterness and anguish the destiny of the people of earth? *Ohuaya, ohuaya.*

But do not anguish, my heart! *Yeehuaya!* Recall nothing now. In truth it hardly gains compassion on this earth. *Yeehuaya!* Truly you have come to increase bitterness at your side, next to you, O Life Giver. *Yyao yyahue auhuayye oo huiya.*

I only look for, I remember my friends. Perhaps they will come one more time, perhaps they will return to life. Or only once do we perish, only one time here on earth? If only our hearts did not suffer! Next to, at your side, Life Giver. *Yyao yyahue auhuayye oo huiya.*

ROMANCES DE LOS SEÑORES #36 (21R-22V)

(Composed when he was fleeing the king of Azcapotzalco, either during his first flight in 1418, when he was 16, or during his second flight, around 1426, when he was 24. This is the earliest poem that may be dated.)

THE FLOWER SONGS

(2)

IN XOCHINQUAHUITL

Xiahuilompehua xiahuiloncuican ticuicanitl huiya ma xonahuiacany, onelelquixtilon ypalnemohuani. Yyeo ayahui ohuaya.

   Ma xonahuiacani ye techonquimiloa ypalnemohua ye xochimaquiztica netotilo ye nehuihuio—Aya!—moxochiuh—A ohuaya—yao yao ho ama y yehuaya ahuayyao aye ohuaya ohuaya. Ye momamana, ye momana ya in tocuic. Maquizcalitec zan teocuitlacalico moyahuan Xochincuahuitl oo. Ye mohui xohua in zan ye motzetzeloa. Ma in tlachichina quetzaltototl ma in tlachichina in zaquan quecholan. Ohuaya.

   Xochincuahuitl timochiuh, timaxelihui, tihuitolihui: o ya timoquetzaco in yehuan. Ixpan timomati tehuan nipapan xochitl. A Ohuaya ohuaya.

   Ma oc xon ya tica oc xon cuepontica yn tlalticpac in. Timolinia tepehui xochitl, timotzetzeloa—Yohuaya ohuaya! Ah tlamiz noxochiuh ah tlamiz nocuic yn noconyayehua—Aaya!—zan nicuicanitl. Huia. Xexelihuiya moyahua yaho cozahua ya xochitl za ye on calaquilo zaquan calitic. A ohuaya ohuaya.

   Yn cacaloxochitl in mayexochitl—Aya ohuaye!—tic ya moyahua, tic ya tzetzeloa xochincalaytec. A ohuaya ohuaya.

   Yyoyahue ye nonocuiltonohua on nitepiltzin niNezahualcoyotl huia nic nechico cozcatl in quetzalin patlahuac ye no nic iximati chalchihuitl. Yaho in tepilhuan. Ohuaya ohuaya. Yxco nontlatlachia nepapan cuauhtli ocelotl, ye no nic yximati chalchiuhtliya in maquiztliya. Ohuaye.

   Tiazque yehua xon ahuiacan. Niquittoa o ni Nezahualcoyotl. Huia! Cuix oc nelli nemohua oa in tlalticpac? Yhui. Ohuaye.

   Annochipa tlalticpac. Zan achica ye nican. Ohuaye ohuaye. Tel ca chalchihuitl no xamani, no teocuitlatl in tlapani, no quetzalli poztequi. Yahui ohuaye. Anochipa tlalticpac zan achica ye nican. Ohuaya ohuaya.

CANTARES MEXICANOS #20 (16V-17R)

(2)

THE FLOWER TREE

Begin the song in pleasure, singer, enjoy, give pleasure to all, even to Life Giver. *Yyeo ayahui ohuaya.*

Delight, for Life Giver adorns us. All the flower bracelets, your flowers, are dancing. Our songs are strewn in this jewel house, this golden house. The flower tree grows and shakes, already it scatters. The quetzal breathes honey, the golden flamingo breathes honey. *Ohuaya, ohuaya.*

You have transformed into a flower tree, you have emerged, you bend and scatter. You have appeared before God's face as multicolored flowers. *Ohuaya, ohuaya.*

Live here on Earth, blossom! As you move and shake, flowers fall. My flowers are eternal, my songs are forever: I raise them: I, a singer. I scatter them, I spill them, the flowers become gold: they are carried inside the golden place. *Ohuaya, ohuyaya.*

Flowers of raven, flowers you scatter, you let them fall in the house of flowers. *Ohuaya, ohuyaya.*

Ah, yes: I am happy, I, prince Nezahualcoyotl, gathering jewels, wide plumes of quetzal, I contemplate the faces of jades: they are the princes! I gaze into the faces of eagles and jaguars, and behold the faces of jades and jewels! Ohuaya ohuyaya.

We will pass away. I, Nezahualcoyotl, say, enjoy! Do we really live on earth? *Ohuaya, ohuaya.*

Not forever on earth, only a brief time here! Even jades fracture; even gold ruptures, even quetzal plumes tear: Not forever on earth: only a brief time here! *Ohuaya, ohuaya.*

CANTARES MEXICANOS #20 (16V-17R)

(3)
A ZAN CHALCHIHUITLI

A zan chalchihuitli quetzal on patlahuac moyollo motlatol totatzin! Ehuaya.
    Tonteicnoitta tonteicnopilitta. In zan cuel achitzin ca in motloc monahuac. Ohuaya ohuaya.
    Chalchiuh itzmolini moxochiuh ipalnemohua. Yexochimimilihui xiuhquechol cuepuntimani. In zan cuel achitzin ca in motloc monahuac! Ohuaya ohuaya.

Romances de los Señores #34 (20v)

(3)

IT IS PURE JADE

It is pure jade, a wide plumage, your heart, your word, O Father! *Ehuaya.*
    You pity man, you watch him with mercy! Only for the most brief moment is he next to you, at your side! *Ohuaya, ohuyaya.*
    Precious as jade your flowers burst forth, O Life Giver. As fragrant flowers they are perfected, as blue parrots they open their corollas. Only for the most brief moment next to you, at your side! *Ohuaya, ohuyaya.*

Romances de los Señores #34 (20v)

(4)

ZAN NOMPEHUA NONCUICA

Zan nompehua noncuica—Aya!—acohui ye noconehua in zan ca ye icuic in ipalnemohua. Yayahue Ohuaya ohuaya.

Cuicailhuizol yecoc hual aciz in Moyocoyatzin in antepilhuan ma on netlanehuilo in cacahuaxochitli. Ahuayya Ohuaya ohuaya.

In ya qui yancohui—Ayahue Huiya!—quen noconchihuaz imaxochitica—Yehuaya!—ma ic ninapantihui ni ya patlaniz ninotolinia ica nichoca. Ohuaya ohuaya.

Cuel achic monahuac—Yehuaya!—ipal nemohuani in ye nelli tonteicuilohua ac at on teicnomati a in tlalticpac? Ohuaya ohuaya.

Nepapan cuauhizhuayoticac in mohuehueuh in ipal nemohua in xochitica celiztica—Ayahue!—ic mitz on ahuiltia a in tepilhuan—Huiya Ohuaya!—achi ye yuhcan in cuicaxochitli huel imanican. Ohuaya ohuaya.

In quetzalizquixochitl on cuepontoc ye oncan—Huiya!—ihcahuaca on tlatohua—Yeehuaya!—in quetzalayacachtototl ipal nemohuani teocuitlaxochitl—Aya!—cuepuntimani—Ya!—achi ye yuhcan in cuicaxochitli huel imanican. Ohuaya ohuaya.

Zan tzinitzcan zacuan ye tlauhquechol ica titlatlapalpohua ye mocuic zan tiquimoquetzaltia in nocnihuan in cuatli ocelo ic tiquim ya melacuahua. Ohuaya ohuaya.

Ac icnopilli naconacitiuh in oncan piltihua mahuiztihua—Yeehuaya!—in mocnihuan in cuauhtli in ocelo ic tiquim melacuahua. Ohuaya ohuaya.

ROMANCES DE LOS SEÑORES #37 (22V-23V)

(4)

I BEGIN TO SING

I begin to sing, I elevate to the heights the song for him by whom all live. *Yayahue ohuaya ohuaya.*

The festive song has arrived: it comes to reach up to the highest arbiter. O lords, borrow precious flowers! *Ahuayya ohuaya ohuaya.*

Already they are being renewed: how will I do it? With your branches I adorn myself, I will fly: I am unfortunate, for that reason I cry. *Ohuaya ohuaya.*

A brief moment at your side, O you by whom all live. Truly you paint the destiny of man. Can you pity the unfortunate here on Earth? *Ohuaya ohuaya.*

With variegated flowers adorned your drum is erected, O you by whom all live. With flowers, with freshness—*Ayahue!*—You give pleasure to the princes. *Huiya ohuaya!* A brief instant in this form is the house of the flowers of song. *Ohuaya ohuaya.*

The beautiful yellow corn flowers open their corollas. *Huiya!* The warbling quetzal of him by whom all live makes a jingling clamor. *Yeehuaya!* Flowers of gold open their corollas. *Aya!* A brief moment in this form is the house of the flowers of the song. *Ohuaya ohuaya.*

With colors of the golden bird, with red-black and lucent red you decorate your songs. With quetzal feathers you ennoble your friends, eagles and jaguars, you make them valiant. *Ohuaya ohuaya.*

Who has the piety to reach above to where it ennobles one, to where it brings glory? *Yehuaya!* Your friends eagles and jaguars, you make them valiant. *Ohuaya ohuaya.*

Romances de los Señores #37 (22v-23v)

(5)
NIC QUETZA TOHUEHUEUH

Nic quetza tohuehueuh niquin nechicohua—Aya!—tocnihuan on in melelquiza niquin cuicatia. Tiyazque ye yuhcan xi quilnamiquican xi ya mocuiltonocan—Aya!—in tocnihuan. Ohuaya ohuaya.

    In cuix oc no ihuiyan canon ye yuhcan—Aya!—cuix oc no ihuiyan canon ximohuayan? Aye ohuaya ohuaya! Ma tihuiyacan, yece ye nican in xochinahuatilo, yece ye nican in cuicanahuatilo tlalticpac. Ehuaya! Xi mocuiltonocan xi moquimilocan a in tocnihuan. Ohuaya ohuaya.

ROMANCES DE LOS SEÑORES #38 (23v-24v)

(5)

I ERECT MY DRUM

I erect my drum, I assemble my friends. *Aya!* Here they find recreation, I make them sing. Thus we must go over there. Remember this. Be happy. *Aya!* Oh, my friends! *Ohuaya ohuaya.*

Perhaps now with calm, and thus it must be over there? *Aya!* Perhaps there is also calm there in the Bodiless Place? *Aye! Ohuaya ohuaya!* Let us go. But here the law of the flowers governs, here the law of the song governs, here on earth. *Ehuaya!* Be happy, dress in finery, O friends. *Ohuaya ohuaya.*

ROMANCES DE LOS SEÑORES #38 (23v-24v)

(6)
TI XIUHTOTOTL

Ti xiuhtototl ti tlauhquechol ti ya patlantinemi. Moyocoya ipal nemohuani: ti mohuihuixohua ya timotzetzelohua nican moqui nochan moqui nocalla imancan. Ohuaya ohuaya.

Monecuiltonol moteicnelil huel ic nemohua in ipal nemohua in tlalticpac: ti mohuihuixohua ya timotzetzelohua nican moqui nochan moqui nocalla imancan. Ohuaya ohuaya.

ROMANCES DE LOS SEÑORES #40 (24V-25R)

(6)

YOU, AZURE BIRD

You, azure bird, shining parrot, you walk flying. O highest arbiter, life giver: trembling, you extend yourself here, filling my house, filling my dwelling here. *Ohuaya ohuaya.*

With your piety and grace one can live, O author of life on Earth: trembling, you extend yourself here, filling my house, filling my dwelling here. *Ohuaya ohuaya.*

Romances de los Señores #40 (24v-25r)

(7)

MELAHUAC XOPANCUICAME

Talpan temoc in xochitl tlalpan, quitemohuia yn ipalnemohuani zaniman—Yehua!—yectli ya xochitl zaniman—Yehua!—cozahuic xochitla. Ohuaya ohuaya.

In maic neapanalo o antepilhuan anteteuctin ayahue ychoquiz tlatelolotihuitza—Aya!—ca quitemohui yn ipalnemoani zaniman yehua yectli ya xochitl zaniman yehua cozahuic xochitla. Ohuaya ohuaya.

Ach tleon i quinequi in toyollo in tlalticpacqui huel teyol quima yn ipalnemoa moxochihuaya ma onnetlanehuilo cozahuic xochitla ca ycahuaca xochitl ayac quicentlamittaz ynic timiquizque. Ahuaye ohuaya.

Intlanel teocuitlatl ma xoyatlatiya intla mochalchiuh mocozqui moquetzal zan tictlanehuico ayac quicentlamittaz ynic timiquizque. Ahuaye ohuaya ohuaya.

Yecan tinemico xochipan tinemico. Ach in tocnihuan, oo, ma iuhcan quentetl ma on nemohua. Ohuaya ohuaya.

In ni Yoyo[tzin] ye nican paqui toyollo, tixco timatico yectli totlatol, antocnihuan yca nichico. Ohuaya ohuaya.

Huixahuee ye ninotolinia icnopilotl—Aya!—in anahuiya in ahuellamati, zan nontlatlcoxtinemi in tlalticpac ye nican. Ohuaya ohuaya.

Ca ya nihuizoc. In quinequi in noyollo yn imahuizon Tiox ho, ipalnemohuani ye oqui piltihua y nica mahuiztihua tlalticpacqui in teucyotl in tlatocayotl. Ohuaya ohuaya.

CANTARES MEXICANOS #82 (69R)

(7)

A PLAIN SPRING SONG

Flowers descend to earth, Life Giver sends them, sacred yellow flowers. *Ohuaya ohuaya.*

Let all be adorned, princes, lords. Life Giver sends them, these wailing piles of sacred flowers, these golden flowers. *Ohuaya ohuaya.*

What do our hearts want on this earth? Heart pleasure. Life Giver, let us borrow your flowers, these golden flowers, these wailing flowers. No one can enjoy them forever, for we must depart. *Ahuaye ohuaya ohuaya.*

Though they may be gold, you will hide them, though they may be your jades, your plumes. We only borrow them. No one can enjoy them forever, for we must depart. *Ahuaye ohuaya ohuaya.*

O friends, to a good place we've come to live, come in springtime! In that place a very brief moment! So brief is life!

I, Yoyontzin, say, Here our hearts are glad. Friends, we have come to know each other and each other's beautiful words. Yet they are also dark. *Ohuaya ohuaya.*

Yes, I suffer, grieve, I am joyless, inconsolable on Earth. *Ohuaya ohuaya.*

I am a hawk. My heart longs for Life Giver God's glory. Here on earth lords are born and they rule through his glory. *Ohuaya ohuaya.*

CANTARES MEXICANOS #82 (69R)

(8)

ZANLO IN XOCHITL TONEQUIMILOL

Zanlo in xochitl tonequimilol, zanio in cuicatl ic huehuetzin telel a in tlalticpac. Ohuaya ohuaya.

In mach noca om polihuiz in cohuayotl, moch noca om polihuiz in icniuhyotl? In ononya yehua ni Yoyontzin. Ohuaye! On cuicatilo in ipalnemoani. Ohuaya ohuaya!

In ma ya moyol iuh quimati in antepilhuan in ancuaht'anmocelo ah mochipan titocnihuan zan cuel achic nican timochi tonyazque o ye ichan. Ohuaya ohuaya.

Nitlayocoya nicnotlamati—Aya!—zan ni tepiltzin ni Nezahualcoyotl—Huiya!—xochitica ihuan cuicatica niquilnamiqui in tepilhuan in oyaque yehuan Tezozomoctzin ihuan Cuahcuauhtzin. A ohuaya ohuaya.

Oc nelli nemoa in Quenonamican: ma ya niquintoca in tepilhuan. Huiya! Ma niquitquili toxochiuh—Aya!—ma itech nonaci yectli yan cuicatl, Tezozomoctzin ihuan Cuahcuauhtzin. A ohuaya ohuaya.

O aic om polihuiz in moteyo nopiltzin ti Tezozomoctzin. Anca zan ye mocuic. O a ica nihualchoca in zan nicnotlamatico zan tiya ehuan. Ohuaya ohuaya.

Zan nihuallayocoya nicnotlamatia ayoc in ayoc in quenmanian titech ya ittaquiuh in tlalticpac in zan tiya ehuan. Ohuaya ohuaya.

CANTARES MEXICANOS #40 (25RV)

(8)

ONLY FLOWERS ARE OUR ADORNMENT

Only flowers are our adornment, only songs turn our suffering to delight on earth. *Ohuaya ohuaya.*

Will I lose my friends and companions? Already I have gone, I, Yoyontzin, to the house of song of he who makes the world live! *Ohuaya ohuaya.*

Let your hearts know, O princes, O eagles and jaguars: not forever will we be friends here: only for a very brief moment and then we all go away to His house. *Ohuaya ohuaya.*

I am sad, I grieve, I, Lord Nezahualcoyotl, when with flowers and songs I remember those princes who went away, Tezozomoc and Cuacuauhtzin. *Ohuaya ohuaya.*

Do they live there still in the realm of mystery? If only I could follow after the princes! Let me carry our flowers and begin the beautiful songs next to Tezozomoc! *Ohuaya ohuaya.*

O my prince Tezozomoc: never will your renown have to end: with a song in your honor I come to suffer and cry: you too have gone away to his house! *Ohuaya ohuaya.*

I come here to feel the sadness, anguish: never more, oh, never more will you come to see us on earth: you too have gone away to his house! *Ohuaya ohuaya.*

CANTARES MEXICANOS #40 (25RV)

(The Tezozomoc addressed in this song is surely not the ruler who ordered his father's death. Tezozomoc was a common name, and the name of a friend and a cousin who died young. On the other hand, the Cuacuauhtzin addressed probably is the same man whose death Nezahualcoyotl caused from love for Azcalxochitzin. Nonetheless, the song seems filled with strange ironies. It must have been composed after 1443, the year of Cuacuauhtzin's death.)

(9)

MAQUIZCUEPONI IN MOXOCHIUH

Maquizcueponi—Ohuaya!—in moxochiuh—Aya!—chalchimmimilihui xochiizhuayo in tomac mani quetzalli yexochitl yece tonequimilol antepilhuan. Huiya Yyayya! Zan tictotlanehuiya in tlalticpac. Ohuaya ohuaya.

    Ma izquixochitli ma cacahuaxochitli neneliuhtimani ye tomac on mani quetzalli yexochitli yece tonequilnilol antepilhuan. Huiya Yyayya! Zan tictotlanehuiya in tlalticpac. Ohuaya ohuaya.

    Zan nihuallaocoya zan nitizahuacihui. Canon tihui ye ichan o ayoc hual ilotihua. Yeehuaya! Cen tihui oc canon tihui. Ohuaya ohuaya.

    Ma itquihuani ichan xochitli cuicatli. Ma ic ninapantihui teocuitlacacal oxochitli quetzalizquixochitli in tomac on mani o ayoc hual ilotihua cen tihui oc canon tihui. Ohuaya ohuaya.

ROMANCES DE LOS SEÑORES #41 (25R-26R)

(9)

AS JEWELS YOUR FLOWERS OPEN THEIR BUDS

As jewels—*Ohuaya!*—your flowers open their buds—*Aya!*—surrounded by emerald foliage. They are in our hands. Precious scented flowers, they are our attire, O princes. We have only borrowed them on earth. *Ohuaya ohuaya.*

Precious and beautiful flowers go away intermingled! They are in our hands. Precious scented flowers, they are our attire, O princes. We have only borrowed them on earth. *Ohuaya ohuaya.*

I sadden, mortally pale. There, from Your house, to where we go: oh, there is no return, no one yet returns here! Once and for all we go away there to where we go! *Ohuaya ohuaya.*

If only we could bring the flowers and the songs to Your house! If only I could go away adorned with golden crow flowers, with beautiful fragrant flowers. In our hands they are now. But oh, there is no return, no one yet returns here! Once and for all we go away there to where we go! *Ohuaya ohuaya.*

Romances de los Señores #41 (25r–26r)

(10)

NI HUALACIC YE NICAN

Ni hualacic ye nican ye ni Yoyontzin—Huiya!—zan nic xochiehelehuia—Yeehuaya!—nixochintlahtlapanaco ya in tlalticpac ye nican noconyatlapana in cacahuaxochitl, nocon ya tlapana icniuhxochitl. In ye tehua monacayo in ti tepiltzin Nezahualcoyotl teuctli Yohyontzin. Yyao ohuili! Yya ayyo yao ayaha! Yohuaya.

Zan nic ya temohuitihuitz mocuic in yectli, ihuan nic ya temohuia in tocnihuan. Aya! Ma on papacohua yehua icniuhtlamachoya. Ya ohuili! Yya ayyo yao ayaha! Yohuaya.

Achin ic nonahuia o achin ic ompahpactinemi noyollo in tlalticpac. Ye ni Yoyontzin nixochehelehuia oo Nixochincuicuicatinemi. Ya ohuaya ohuaya.

Nic nehnequi nic ehelehuia in icniuyotl in tecpillotl nixochehelehuia oo Nixochincuicuicatinemi. Ya ohuaya.

O anca yuhqui in chalchihuitl—Ohuaya!—zan ca yuhqui in cozcatl in quetzalli patlahuac ipan ye nicmatia yectli ye mocuic—Aya!—ipalnemoani ica nonahuia ica nonnitotiya huehuetitlan oo xopan cala itic in ye ni Yohyontzin. Huiya! Ha noyol quimati. Ohuaya ohuaya.

Ma xic huel in tzotzona moxochihuehueuh ticuicanitl. Iyehuaya! Ma izquixochitl in ma cacahuaxochitl in ma on moyahua—Aya!—ma on tzetzelihui ye nican huehuetitlan oo. Ma in tahuiyacan. Ohuaya ohuaya.

Ya zan ca xiuhquechol tzinizcan tlauhquechol oncan on cuicatlatohua ya in xochitl ic paqui. Hoo alilili yao ayyaha ohuaya ohuaya.

A oncan ya ihcac in Xochincuahuitl in huehuetitlan. Ayahue! Zan ye itech on nemi ya in quetzalin quechol in tototl ipan mochiuhtinemi o in Nezahualcoyotzin o in xochitl ic paqui. Hoo alilili yao ayyaha ohuaya ohuaya.

CANTARES MEXICANOS #25 (18V-19R)

(10)

I HAVE ARRIVED HERE

I have arrived here, I, Yoyontzin, yearning only for flowers, cutting flowers on the earth, cocoa flowers, cut flowers of friendship, which are your body, O prince. Lord Nezahualcoyotl I am, Yoyontzin. *Yyao ohuili yya ayyo yao ayya yohuiya.*

I only come bringing your beautiful songs, I carry them down, finding friends. Be joyful here, let your friendship be revealed. *Yyao ohuili yya ayyo yao ayya yohuiya.*

I take delight a brief time, only fleetingly is my heart glad on earth. I, Yoyontzin: I yearn for flowers. *Ohuaya ohuaya.*

I live with flowery songs. I want and desire deep brotherhood, nobility. I yearn for songs: I live in flowery songs. *Ohuaya ohuaya.*

As jade, as jewels, as a wide plumage of quetzal, I value your song, Giver of Life, with these I take enjoyment, with them I dance between the drums in the flowery house of spring. I, Yoyontzin, my heart enjoys it. *Ohuaya ohuaya.*

Sound your flower drum beautifully, singer; scatter perfumed corn flowers, chocolate flowers, they are spilled as rain here next to the drums. Let us enjoy them. *Ohuaya ohuaya.*

Already the long-necked turquoise bird, the black trogon, the red parrot sing and warble there, joyful with the flowers. *Yao ayyaha ohuaya ohuaya.*

Already the flower tree is raised there next to the drum. The precious red bird is in it: Nezahualcoyotl has become a bird, joyful being with flowers. *Yao ayyaha ohuaya ohuaya.*

CANTARES MEXICANOS #25 (18V-19R)

(11)

TZINITZCAXUCHITLA IHUA QUIMALINA

Tzinitzcaxuchitla ihua quimalina in yectli yan cuicatl ic tonteyapanaco ticuicanitli—Huiya!—Ic tontequimilohua nepapan xochitli. Ma ic xon ahuiyacan in antepilhuan. Ohuaya ohuaya.

Cuix oc yuh nemohua canon ye yuh quenonamican? Canin cuix oc ahuiyalo? A ca zaniyo nican tlalticpac xochitica ya hual iximacho cuicatica ya ye on tlaneuh ti tocnihuan. Ohuaya ohuaya.

Ma moxochiuh ica xi mapana in tlauhquechol xochitl—Aya!—tonatimania in cacaloxochitli ma ica titoquimilocan tlalticpac ye nican yece ye nican. Ohuaya ohuaya.

In zan achitzinca in ma ihui cuel achic on netlanehuilo ixochiuh—Ayehuaye!—ya itquihui in ichan ihua ximohuacan no ye ichan auh in amo zan ic on polihui in tellel in totlaocol. Ohuaya ohuaya.

ROMANCES DE LOS SEÑORES #39 (24RV)

(11)

WITH BLACK FLOWERS AND STRIPES OF GOLD

With black flowers and stripes of gold you interlace the beautiful song. With it you, singer, come to adorn the people. *Huiya!* With a spectrum of flowers you dress the people. Enjoy! *Ohuaya ohuaya.*

Perhaps like this the dead live now, beyond, in the place of mystery? Is there perhaps pleasure there? Or is it only here on earth? With flowers knowledge is given, with flowers one is shown, O my friend! *Ohuaya ohuaya.*

Regale yourself with flowers, shining macaw flowers, brilliant like the sun; with flowers of the crow let us regale ourselves on the earth, here but only here. *Ohuaya ohuaya.*

Only a brief instant will it be thus: for a very brief time you are lent your flowers. Already they are carried to their house, to the Bodiless Place, which is also your house. Is this not so? With this knowledge, our sadness and bitterness perish. *Ohuaya ohuaya.*

ROMANCES DE LOS SEÑORES #39 (24RV)

(12)

TEPONAZCUICATL

Titoco titoco titocoti

Niquetzal xochiatototl ilhuizol mana. Aya! Nicuicatl ilhuicatl Anahuac, on nemi—Aya!—noyollo tlacatempan, a nic moyahua ya noxochiuh—Aya!—ica yehua ihuintihua tepilhuan. Oo, nequimilolo, Yaya ye yahao.

Nicnotlamatia, yaya yaha ohua. Zan nentlamati noyol, nicuicanitl chiuhnahuatl itempan xochitlalpan. Ya nicnihuan ma ya huiyelo—Aya! —niquilolo. Ya oncan yehuaya.

Chalchiuhtli ololohuic a nicnocozcatia, nicuicanitl ye nomacehual. Ayehuaya! chalchiuhtli in popoca zan nictimaloa cuicatl —Aya!—quihuinti ye noyol xochintlalticpac on nequimilolo. Ya oncan yehuaya.

Zan noncuica nentlamati in tlalticpac. Aya! Ni cuicanitl, Ohuaye, tan iticpa quiza notlayocol—Aya!—cuicatl. Aya! Quihuinti ye noyol xochintlalticpac on nequimilolo. Ye oncan yehuaya. Aya.

Toltecayotl ye nicuilohuitehuaz, nicuicanitl nocuicayo nemiz a in tlalticpac, cuicatl ica nilnamicoz ohua nipinohuan, niaz nipoliuhitiuh cozcatozpetlac ninotecatiuh chochotiaz nononanhuan ixayotl pixauhtiaz notomio oloxochio nitepehui. Cocahuicatl itempan, o ca yehua. Ayahue aya.

Aye aya ohuaye! Nicnotlamati amopinohuan, ihuipetlacotl nihuicaloni canin Tlapalla poctlan tihuatoc. Ompa yan noyaz niyaz nipoliuhtiuh, cozcapetlac ninotecatiuh, chochotiaz nononanhuan.

CANTARES MEXICANOS #50 (31RV)

(12)

TEPONAZTLI DRUM SONG

Drum: titoco titoco titocoti

I, a quetzal feather, a bird of the flowering water, I flow in celebration. I am a song. In the wide wall of the water, my heart walks on the lips of the men. I am beautifying my flowers; with them the princes become intoxicated. There is adornment. *Yayaye yahao.*

I suffer, ay, my heart is desolate, I, a poet on the Shore of the Nine Currents. In the world of flowers, take pleasure, all of you, O my friends; already it is time to be adorned. *Yahueha.*

I put on a necklace of round jades, I, a singer, these are my payments. The jades sparkle, I exalt them in my song. They enrapture my heart. Let all be adorned in this flower world.

When I, a singer, sing on earth, my inner sadness departs. They enrapture my heart. Let all be adorned in the flower world beyond. *Yahue aya.*

I will leave a work of painted art. I, a singer whose songs will live on earth: with songs I will be remembered, O warriors, I will go away, I will disappear, I will be strewn on a mat of jewels and yellow feathers. The old women will cry for me. Their wails will drain my bones; as a flowery log I will be scattered there on the shore of the doves. *Aya ohuaya.*

Ayao ata ohuaye. Warriors, I suffer. I'm carried along on a canopy of feathers. In Tlapallan, smoke will disperse. I will go there, I will disappear, strewn on a mat of jewels and yellow feathers.

CANTARES MEXICANOS #50 (31RV)

(13)

ICUIC NEZAHUALCOYOTZIN

Totoco totoco tico totoco totoco. Ic ontlantiuh: tico titico titico tico

Nican ya quetzaco tohuehueuh. Ao! Niquimitotia cuauhtloocelo. In ca tiya ihcac in cuicaxochitl. Nic temoa a in cuicatl ye tonequimilol. Ayyo.
    Quiyo quiyonca. Aya. Nichoca. Aya! Ni Nezahualcoyotl. Huiya! Quen ni ye nonyaz o ya nipolihuiz oya Miquitlan? Ye ni mitz cahua noteouh ipalnemoa ti nech nahuatia ye niaz nipolihuiz oya Miquitlan. Ayyo.
    Quen on maniz tlalli in Acolihuacan? Huiya! Cuix oc quenman o ticmomoyahuaz in momacehual? Ye mitz cahua noteouh ipalnemoa. Ti nech nahuatia ye niaz nipolihuiz oya Miquitlan. Ayyo.
    Zanio cuicatl tonequimilol, quipoloa—Aya!—in totlacuilolli tepilhuan, oo. Ma ya ahuilihua nican. Aya! Ayac ichan in tlalticpac, oo. Tic ya cencahuazque huelic yexochitl. Ayyo.

Quititi quititi quiti quiti tocoto tocoti tocototocoti. Zan ic mocueptiuh.

Ma xochicuico—Aya!—ma ihtoa nic huana—Ayyahue!—teihuinti xochitl. Ahuaya! Yehcoc ye nican poyoma, xa huallan timaliuhtihuitz. Ayyo.
    Maxochitl o yehcoc ye nican. Ayyahue! Zan tlaahuixochitla moyahua—Aya!—motzetzeloa an ca to yehuatl nepapan xochitl. Ayyo! Zan comoni huehuetl ma ya nehtotilo. Ayyo.
    In quetzalpoyomatl a ic icuilihuic noyol, nicuicanitl in xochitl a ya tzetzelihui ipan cuel nicuiya. Ma xon ahuiacan. Ayyo! Zan noyolitic on tlapani in cuicaxochitl nic ya moyahua in xochitla. Ayyo.
    Cuicatl ya ninoquimilotehuaz in quenmanian, xochineneliuhtiaz noyollo, yehuan tepilhuan on teteuctin in. Ayyo.
    Zan ye ic nichoca in quenmanian, zan nic aya ihtoa noxochiteyo nocuicatoca, nic tlalitehuaz in quenmanian, xochineneliuhtiaz noyollo, yehuan tepilhuan in tetecutin in. Ayyo.

Tico toco tocoto. Ic ontlantiuh: ticoto ticoto.

Toztli yan quechol nipatlantinemia in tlalla icpac oquihuinti. Ye noyol. Ahuayyai.
    Niquetzaltototl niyecoya ye iquiapan yceltcotl y xochiticpac nihueloncuica oo nicuicaihtoa paqui. Ye noyol. Ahuayyai.
    Xochiatl in pozontimania yn tlalla icpac oquihuinti. Ye noyol. Ahuayyai.

(13)

SONG OF NEZAHUALCOYOTL

Drums: Totoco totoco tico totoco totoco. At the end: tico titico titico tico

Our drums are ready; already I inspire the eagles and jaguars to dance. Already you are on your feet, song flower. I search for songs, our adornments. *Ayyo.*

Toward the end of it all I, Nezahualcoyotl, go weeping. Why must I go lose myself in the land of the dead? Already I leave you, by whom all live, you command me to lose myself in the land of the dead. *Ayyo.*

How will things continue on Earth, in Acolhuacan? In time will you disperse all your dependents, spirit of all I leave behind?

Only songs are our adornments. Already He destroys our painted books, the princes. Be joyful here, no one has his house on earth; we must leave the fragrant flowers. *Ayyo.*

Drums: Quititi quititi quiti quiti tocoto tocoti tocototocoti. Just thus it will come back in.

Let there be flower songs. Let my younger brothers sing. I drink intoxicating flowers; already they have arrived, the flowers that make us dizzy, they come to glorify. *Ayyo.*

Let there be flowers. Bouquets of flowers have already arrived here; flowers of pleasure are scattered, many-colored flowers rain entwined. The drum resounds: let the dance begin. *Ayyo.*

I, the singer, plumes of narcotic flowers tint my heart; already I scatter flowers, they are quickly taken. Enjoy. Within my heart the song flowers burst, already I scatter flowers. *Ayyo.*

With songs I must deck m+yself, with flowers my heart must be entwined: they are princes, they are kings! *Ayyo.*

For this I cry sometimes and say: The fame of my flowers, the renown of my songs, I will leave abandoned someday: with flowers my heart must be entwined: they are princes, they are kings! *Ayyo.*

Drums: Tico toco tocoto. At the end: ticoto ticoto.

As a parrot, as a quechol bird, I fly above the earth, my heart drunk. *Ahuayyai.*

I am a quetzal, I arrive in the One Spirit's place of rain, beautifully over the flowers; singing, my heart fills with joy. *Ahuayyai.*

Flowers flood the earth: my heart is drunk. *Ahuayyai.*

Ninochoquilia niquinotlamati ayac inchan on tlallicpac Ahuayyai.
    Zan niquittoaya ye niMexicatl ma niyahuiya nohtlatoca tequantepec niyahui polihuin chiltepehua—Aya!—ye choca in tequantepehua. Ohuaye ohuaya.
    Maca qualania nohueyo yehua Mexicatli polihui chil. Ahuayyai!
    Citlalin in popocaya ipan ye moteca y za ye polihuia zan ye xochitecatl. Ohuaye Ahuayyai! Zan yechocaya Amaxtecatl aya ca ye chocaya tequantepehua. Ahuayyai.

Toto tiquiti tiquiti. Ic ontlantiuh: tocotico tocoti tototitiqui tototitiquiti

Oyamoquetz huehuetl ooon ma annetotilo teteuctin—Aya!—ma onnetlanehuihuilo chalchihuitl on quetzal i patlahuac ayac ychan tlalticpac. Ayio! Zan nomac onmania ooo yxochiuh—Aya!—ipalnemoa ma onnetlanchuilo chalchihuitl.
    Oyohualin colinia oon in icelteotl ipalnemoa anahuac o onnemia noyol. Ayio.
    Yn yancuica oncan quixima ipalnemoani ca ye Nonoalco ahuilizapani in teuctli yehua Nezahualpilli y yece ye oncan—Aya!—in tlacochtenanpan atlixco. Ayio! Zan momac otitemic motlahua' zomal a ica ticahuiltia ycelteotl in teuctli yehua. Ayio.
    Yyeho aye icnotlamati noyollo zan Ninonoalcatl zan can nicolintototl o nocamapan—Aya!—Mexicatl. Yn cayio.
    Onquetzalpipixauhtoc motlachinolxochiuh yn ipalnemoa zan ca nicoli. Yn cayio.

Toco toco tiqui tiqui. Ic ontlantiuh: tocotico tocoti.

Ma ya pehualoya nicuihua In ma ya oncuico ye nicaan—Aya oya!— ye'coc yehuan dios—Yn cayio!—in ma ycaya onahuilihuan tepilhuan a—Aya!—mocuic—Oya!—yehuan dios oncan titemoc yehuan dios a oncan huelin oncan tlacat y ye... Yn cayio!
    In oncan tlahuizcalli milintimani mochan—Aya!—moxochiuh aya chalchiuhcueponi maquiztzetzelihui on netlamachtiloya—In cayio!—Yn oncan yao nepapan izhuayo moxochiuh—Aya!—dios. In cayio.
    Zan ye xochitl moyahua oo zan ca ytlatol yn ipalnemoani oon tepan ye moteca anahuac oo yca tichuelmana atlon yan tepetl. Ayio.
    Zan te momac mania cemanahuatl in niman ye tehuatl toconyaittoaya ipalnemoani.

CANTARES MEXICANOS #46 (28V - 29R)

I cry and grieve, for no one has a home on earth. *Ahuayyai.*

I, a Mexica, say, let me have pleasure as I march to Tecuantepec: I go to destroy the Chiltepecans, so the Tecuantepecans may weep.

If only these warriors of mine, these Mexicas, were not so warlike! They destroy! *Ahuayyai.*

A comet showers down upon them. Perished are the Xochitecans, weeping are the Amaxtecans, weeping are the Tecuantepecans. *Ahuayyai.*

Drums: Toto tiquiti tiquiti. At the end: tocotico tocoti tototitiqui tototitiquiti

The drums have begun; now let the dancing start, lords, put on your fine jades, wear the broad feathers that you borrow. No one has a house on this earth! Already I hold the flowers of Life Giver, the borrowed jades.

Life Giver, the Creator, is shaking his rattles; in Anahuac my heart is thrilled. *Ayio.*

There, in Nonoalco, the Place Beyond, the Water Place, on the flood crest grasping his spear-thrower, Lord Nezahualpilli appears. Life Giver brings him down once more. *Ayio.*

Grasp your spear-thrower, Lord. This gives the One Spirit pleasure. *Ayio.*

My heart grieves, I am a Nonoalcan, a quail who speaks Mexica. *In cayio.*

My feathers fall like mist, my burning flowers, O Life Giver, I am a quail. *In cayio.*

Drums: Toco toco tiqui tiqui. At the end: tocotico tocoti

Brothers, let it now begin, let there be music. *Aya, oya*! God has arrived! Now let there be pleasure because of these songs, these princes. O God, you've descended from beyond, born beyond, beyond. *In cayio.*

In your home beyond, dawn is woven; your flowers, your songs bloom like jades, their petals fall like bracelets from the place where one knows joy, from beyond, your many flowers and leaves, O God. *In cayio.*

These flowers, scattered words of Life Giver, shower down on Anahuac. With these you make the city endure. *Ayio.*

Your hands are the world. It is you who sees, O Life Giver.

Cantares Mexicanos #46 (28v - 29r)

The Life of Hungry Coyote

(1402-1472)

Nezahualcoyotl. Codex Azcatitlan.

Ce Mazatl Acolmiztli Nezahualcoyotl was born on the day 1 Deer in the year 1 Rabbit, or April 28, 1402. He was the first legitimate son of the Texcocan ruler Ixtlilxochitl and his queen, Matlalcihuatzin, an Aztec princess. His blood joined the peoples of Texcoco with Tenochtitlan, which was to became his second home. Acolmiztli, his original given name, means "Shoulder of Puma." Later he received the name Nezahualcoyotl, Hungry Coyote, during his hard years in exile. He was also known by the astrological day of his birth, Ce Mazatl, 1 Deer, and the nickname Yoyontzin. He had many siblings and half-siblings.

Somewhere between the ages of six and eight, he started attending the *calmecac* school, where noble children were sent. There the foremost Aztec scholar of his time, Huitzilihuitzin, took him under his wing and taught him the history and wisdom of the Toltecs. The *calmecac* was presided over by the Toltec deity Quetzalcoatl, while the *telpochcaltin* schools, which the majority of the population attended, were presided over by the patron deity of the city, Tezcatlipoca. Quetzalcoatl and Tezcatlipoca were in many ways opposites and opponents, yet they also formed a strange unity, a dynamic dichotomy that worked itself out in the society and was to play an essential role in Hungry Coyote's life.

Originally, Hungry Coyote's metropolis of Texcoco, which means "Place of Rest," had been founded by a wandering Chichimec people who called themselves the Alcolhuans and were hunters and nomads from the desert, formerly living in caves and wearing animal skins. They arrived about the year 1000 at Lake Texcoco. The Alcolhuans settled there, receiving permission from Xolotl, the Chichimec overlord of the region, who had taken over hegemony of the Valley of Mexico after the fall of the Toltecs of Tula.

One branch of the Toltecs' own ancestors had also been Chichimec nomads, immigrating from the north a century earlier into the area where Teotihuacan's great civilization had once flourished. Although Teotihuacan was deserted when they arrived, many of the descendants of people who had dispersed from that great city still lived in towns nearby, while others had moved further on, notably to Cholula. By living near them over a period of time and intermarrying, these rough Chichimecs became the sophisticated Toltecs of Tula, the inheritors of Teotihuacan's culture. In Nahuatl, *toltecatl* means a craftsman, artist, or engineer.

A century later, Hungry Coyote's Alcolhuan ancestors went through a similar process of transformation. The same civilizing forces continued at work in the Valley of Mexico. Near the spot where the Alcolhuans began to build Texcoco was a small community of Toltec refugees from Tula. Learning the ways of civilization from them, the Alcolhuans soon shed their animal skins for cotton clothing, their nomadic ways for farming and village life.

Through several generations, the Alcolhuan chiefs adopted Toltec-Teotihuacan culture as their own. Under Xolotl's grandson, the Chichimecs changed from a hunting to an agricultural people. The succeeding ruler, Quinatzin, moved the Chichimec capital from Xolotl's Tenayuca across the lake to Texcoco. Thus Texcoco became the political center of the region. The fifth ruler, Techotlala, Hungry Coyote's grandfather, decreed that their official tongue would no longer be their rough Chichimec language, but the silvery Nahuatl of ancient Tula. He summoned learned scribes from the land of the Mixtecs, where the Toltec arts had been highly preserved, to teach them hieroglyphic book painting. The Texcocans began to follow the Toltec religion, taking Quetzalcoatl as their cultural divinity, while integrating their old tribal deities into Tezcatlipoca, the patron of the military orders. The dichotomy of Quetzalcoatl and Tezcatlipoca, peace and war, day and night, opposites in an eternal struggle but forming a strange unity, runs through Mexican history. The history of Texcoco, like Tula before it, was swept up in this struggle.

While the little Alcolhuan settlement was busy growing into the metropolis of Texcoco, on the opposite lake bank another wandering desert people arrived, the Mexica or Tenochca, known to us as the Aztecs. They too took Nahuatl as their new mother tongue and began their own city, Tenochtitlan, on a barren island across the lake ten miles away. While the Aztecs were still struggling with survival, the Texcocans were the dominant force in the region and were becoming a high culture.

At the same time, a third center was growing powerful, the Tepaneca city of Azcapotzalco, ruled by another branch of Xolotl's imperial Toltec lineage. Azcapotzalco, not far from Tenochtitlan, became the dominant city on the west side of the lake and held the Aztecs as a subject people.

When Hungry Coyote was eleven, his grandfather died. A struggle ensued between his father, Ixtlilxochitl, and the ruler of Azcapotzalco, Tezozomoc, over who had the right to succession in the line of Xolotl as the next Great Chichimetl, the supreme ruler.

The Texcocan army surrounded and sieged Azcapotzalco for four years. Finally Tezozomoc sued for peace, agreeing to recognize Ixtlilxochitl as supreme ruler. Texcoco's army quickly disarmed but soon as their guard was down, Azcapotzalco attacked, with help from Tenochtitlan. This happened in the year 4 Rabbit, or 1418, when Hungry Coyote was sixteen years old. Ixtlilxochitl was caught unprepared. Texcoco held out for fifty days, but finally Ixtlilxochitl, Hungry Coyote, and the rest of his family fled. The Tepanecas pursued.

Nezahualcoyotl in a tree watches his father's death. Codex Xolotl.

THE LIFE OF HUNGRY COYOTE

47

Leaving the rest of the family hiding in a nearby forest, Ixtlilxochitl, Hungry Coyote, and two Texcocan captains climbed down a deep gorge, followed by enemy soldiers. As the enemy approached, Ixtlilxochitl ordered Hungry Coyote to hide in a tree. From that vantage point he watched his father fight to the death. The Tepanecas left him where he fell. When they were gone, Hungry Coyote cremated his father's body in accordance with Toltec ritual.

Tezozomoc offered a reward for Hungry Coyote's capture dead or alive, but, with help from his great-uncle Itzcoatl, who was destined to become the Aztec ruler, Hungry Coyote escaped over the hills to Tlaxcala, where he had relatives and friends. He did not stay in one place long, but moved around the various nearby city-states. Already a poet, he composed "Song of the Flight" while in exile. There are many stories of this period filled with danger and narrow escapes.

To stamp out a budding revolt in Texcoco, Tezozomoc sent soldiers asking every child in the region who the king was. Those who answered Ixtlilxochitl or Hungry Coyote were killed. He made Hungry Coyote's own brother, Tilmatzin, puppet governor of Texcoco and instituted annual tribute payments. He dismantled Texcoco's realm, dividing up the land among bordering states, each governed by one of his allies. Texcoco itself he gave to Tenochtitlan. Tezozomoc and his harsh regime became increasingly hated.

Hungry Coyote lay low for six years. Finally several of his aunts convinced Tezozomoc to permit him to come out of hiding and live in Tenochtitlan, arguing that the threat had passed. Hungry Coyote spent the next two years there quietly working as a builder. He found he had a genius for construction, creating the park at Chapultepec and engineering an aqueduct from it to Tenochtitlan, alleviating the city's fresh water shortage. At the end of that period, those same aunts convinced Tezozomoc to grant Hungry Coyote permission to return to Texcoco. His presence there, they claimed, would help support the regime.

Back home in Texcoco at last, Hungry Coyote stayed out of politics and seemed to be living the life of an idle young lord. But as Tezozomoc aged, he became concerned that Hungry Coyote might challenge his choice of succession, seeing that his abilities and personality had won him many friends. Rather than attack him openly, Tezozomoc arranged several plots on his life, all of which were foiled.

As Tezozomoc approached death, he named a young son as successor, passing over his eldest son, Maxtla. At the public declaration of the new emperor, Maxtla stopped the proceedings and claimed the throne. He killed his brother, as well as the rulers of Tenochtitlan and Tlaltelolco, and sent his men to kill Hungry Coyote. Once again Hungry Coyote fled the city and went into hiding. Another price was put on his head.

From the mountains Hungry Coyote began to organize rebellion, slowly forging an alliance of Texcocan exiles with many of the neighboring city-states, Tlaxcala, Huexotzingo, Cholula, Chalco, and others. Their combined armies routed Maxtla's garrisons on the east side of the lake, and, on August 11, 1427, at the age of 25, Hungry Coyote led his triumphant followers into Texcoco.

But Maxtla still dominated the west side of the lake, with Tenochtitlan still under his control. Hungry Coyote forged a secret alliance with his great-uncle Itzcoatl, who had become ruler of Tenochtitlan. With the smaller city of Tlacopan, their Triple Alliance attacked Azcapotzalco by land and by canoe. After a campaign of one hundred fifteen days, the Tepaneca capital was burned and Maxtla was dead.

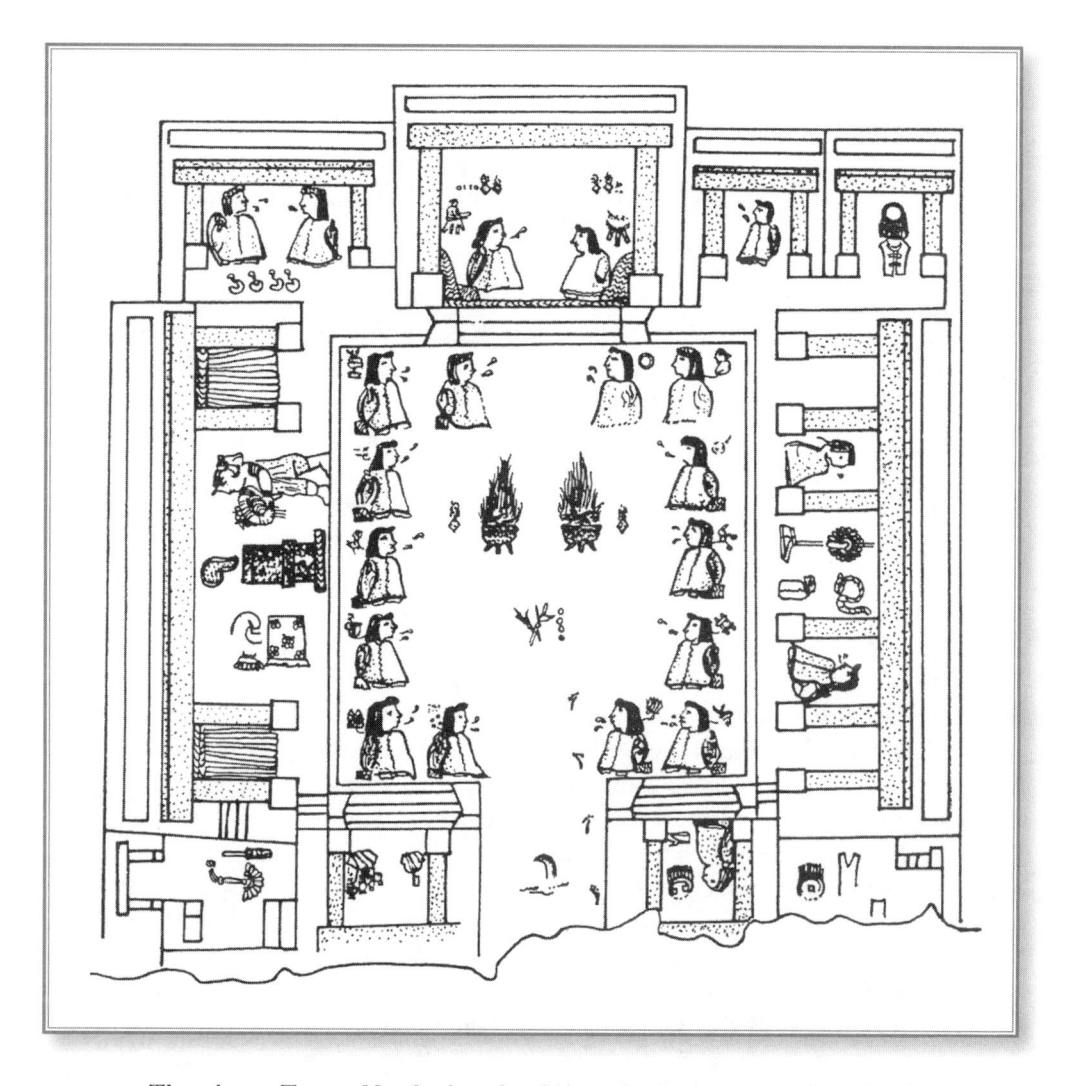

The palace at Texcoco. Nezahualcoyotl and his son in the throne room (top middle). In the courtyard are two perpetual fires. The hall of science and music is left of the courtyard; storehouse to the right; judges' chambers top left. Mapa Quinatzin.

Crowned supreme ruler (*tlacatecuhtli*) by his people, Hungry Coyote set to work to rebuild his shattered city. Under his leadership, Texcoco rose from destruction and reached heights of culture not seen in the Valley of Mexico since the fall of Tula. Toltec learning, after an eclipse of generations, blossomed again in Texcoco and instigated a cultural renaissance in the entire Valley of Mexico.

At the very heart of Texcoco, Hungry Coyote placed an innermost courtyard surrounded by a square of buildings housing the council chambers and halls of justice, and quarters for himself and for four hundred other chiefs, scholars, artists, historians, philosophers, musicians, and poets. In a large hall nearby was the university, whose library of hieroglyphic *amoxtli* books was the greatest on the continent (later burned by Cortés).

He promoted the arts, sciences, and humanities: astronomy, calendrics, engineering, architecture, history, philosophy, law, sculpture, painting, music, song, and poetry. He saw that they recorded and preserved their knowledge in the great library.

Hungry Coyote's engineering genius made it possible for Texcoco and Tenochtitlan to become great metropolises. He engineered the first aqueduct to bring fresh water from Teotihuacan to Texcoco, as he had already done from Chapultepec to Tenochtitlan, and watered the fields with canals. He planted a park with a thousand cypresses. He devised and built a dike that stretched across the entire lake, separating the brackish water of the northeast from the fresh water of the southwest. Before that, during flood years salt water had often ruined the harvests at the *chinampas* of the floating gardens of Xochimilco.

Hungry Coyote devised a code of eighty laws, the first codification of the law in the Valley of Mexico, which covered property rights, criminal activities, and morality, harsh by our standards but so comprehensive and concise that all the other Nahua city-states adopted the code as their own. He organized a form of government by councils. The Council of Justice, the supreme court of the land, had seats reserved for common citizens.

The Council of Music was directed to encourage art and science, and its members would meet regularly to exchange information and teach. Hungry Coyote paid the teaching fees for orphans. On certain days, new works of poetry and history were presented before the council by their authors. Goldsmiths, feather workers, poets, and musicians would receive prizes for achievements and punishments for bad craftsmanship.

There was also a school of divination art. In the innermost courtyard at the very center of Texcoco, the philosopher-poets debated in "the dialog of the songs." The Council of Justice awarded prizes for merit, while the willful falsification of historical truth was punishable by death. That harsh punishment was in response to what had happened in Tenochtitlan, where the emperor had ordered all history books destroyed and history rewritten in order to better legitimize his branch of the Aztec dynasty as heirs to the Toltecs.

Hungry Coyote saw that widows and aged and wounded soldiers were taken care of with food and clothing from the royal storehouses. He opened the forests to permit the poor to gather dry wood for their fires, which had been forbidden. During times of drought he opened the royal storehouses to all people in need.

A sensuous man, Hungry Coyote had numerous concubines and children by them but approached the age of forty without ever having married, and so he had no heir apparent. Feeling loveless, he fell into a great melancholy. One day while walking along the lake shore in this sad state he met Cuacuauhtzin, the governor of a small neighboring city, who invited him home to dinner, where a young woman named Azcalxochitzin served their table. Hungry Coyote was so taken by her charm and beauty that all sadness left him and he realized that she possessed his heart. However, she was Cuacuauhtzin's betrothed. Crazed with desire, Hungry Coyote ordered Cuacuauhtzin to be sent into battle against their perennial rival, Tlaxcala. He fought there and died. Hungry Coyote took Azcalxochitzin as his wife. The following three years were filled with drought and plagues of locusts, which Hungry Coyote took as punishment for his transgression.

It was not long before the question arose over whether Texcoco or Tenochtitlan would be the dominant city-state in the region. Tenochtitlan had swelled to double Texcoco's population of about 150,000. That clearly tipped the balance toward the Aztecs, together

Nezahualcoyotl, Azcalxochitzin, and two artist-scribes. Mapa Tlotzin.

with the militancy they had developed as they rose from slaves to masters. When his great-uncle Itzcoatl died and Moctezuma I succeeded him as ruler of Tenochtitlan, Hungry Coyote journeyed there and proposed a continuation of their alliance. The Aztec council replied that the price of peace would be Texcoco's recognizing the primacy of the Aztecs. Hungry Coyote handled the situation with statesmanship and arranged a fake war. The two armies met on a field and exchanged ritual insults. The Texcocan army retreated, and a small Aztec force followed to the outskirts of Texcoco. Hungry Coyote himself set a symbolic fire to the temple atop the main pyramid in Texcoco. Thus the Aztecs gained recognition as the dominant power of the region, and no one was hurt.

But with the rise of Tenochtitlan came an obsession with heart sacrifice, which involved cutting out the victim's heart and offering it, still beating, to a deity, usually one associated with war. The cult of sacrifice, intimately connected with the Aztec warrior orders, spread as the Aztec ascendancy spread throughout the entire Nahua world. The Aztec cult made inroads into Texcoco. A temple to the war god Huitzilopochtli was begun in the center of Hungry Coyote's city.

Peace, or at least order, had come to the entire Valley of Mexico and beyond, where the Triple Alliance now ruled largely unchallenged. Wars became increasingly distant as the empire expanded. Yet despite the triumph and ascendancy of the Aztecs, the inner contradictions of their society eventually came to a head. Peacetime proved a less than convenient event, as many of their social structures had been built around war. The Aztec warrior orders flourished in war, though it became increasingly difficult to find city-states willing to confront the Triple Alliance juggernaut. Warriors were rewarded with the highest honors, and those who met death on the field of battle were believed to live eternally in the fields of the sun. A new generation was recruited into the warrior orders, but they complained of too few situations in which to test their skills or win glory. According to the creation myths of the priests of the warrior orders, the priests of Tezcatlipoca and Huitzilopochtli, the world had been created and the sun made to move by the sacrificial deaths of the deities. The priests of the warrior orders believed that it was the God-given mission of the Aztecs to keep this world alive by ritual blood sacrifice in re-creation of that myth, and for that they needed prisoners of war.

Terrible floods and unseasonable frosts devastated the region in the year 10 Rabbit or 1450, followed by a great drought and famine. Nezahualcoyotl did all he could to succor his people, distributing the reserves of corn from the state granaries. But the calamities seemed endless. The year 1 Rabbit or 1454 began with a full eclipse of the sun. The rulers of the Triple Alliance held a summit conference to discuss the best remedy. The priests of Tezcatlipoca and Huitzilopochtli from Tenochtitlan cried that the gods were angry that there were not enough captives to sacrifice and demanded more. In former times, they claimed, when they did not have enough captives they would sacrifice their own sons and slaves.

Hungry Coyote was strongly opposed, arguing that it always used to be enough to sacrifice captives of war and, since these would have died in battle otherwise, no further lives were lost; besides, it was a great feat for a soldier to capture a live enemy. The priests argued that the current wars were very remote and that the captives who arrived back in Tenochtitlan were too few and too debilitated.

As a solution, the Triple Alliance instituted the War of the Flowers, staging combat every twenty days with Tlaxcala, Huexotzinco, and Cholula, "the enemies within the house," to capture prisoners for sacrifice and to provide a venue where young warriors could gain glory. The battles did not extend beyond the limits of the field, so neither land nor political dominion was at stake.

Hungry Coyote had witnessed death and sacrifice throughout his life and had become increasingly sickened by it. He had always struggled with the sacrificial priests of "black" Tezcatlipoca by promoting Quetzalcoatl, the Giver of Life (also known as the "white" Tezcatlipoca). Now he also had to deal with the Aztec priests of Huitzilopochtli, who were far more devoted to the heart sacrifice than the priests of the "black" Tezcatlipoca had ever been. He found himself in the same situation that the legendary Toltec *tlatoani* Quetzalcoatl-Topiltzin had been in during an earlier epoch in the city of Tula, when Quetzalcoatl-Topiltzin had fought Tezcatlipoca-Huemac over the issue of blood sacrifice. That struggle had resulted in the exile of Quetzalcoatl-Topiltzin and the destruction of Tula, and Hungry Coyote did not want this struggle to destroy Texcoco.

Instead of the weapons of war, Hungry Coyote struggled using the weapons of poetry and music. He stopped attending the blood sacrifices. At the dedication ceremony of Huitzilopochtli's temple in the year 1 Reed (1467) he performed a poem in which he prophesied the temple's destruction in another 1 Reed, when the Aztec calendar repeated its fifty-two-year cycle.

IN A YEAR SUCH AS THIS

In a year such as this, this now new temple will be destroyed. Who will be present? My son or grandson?

Then the earth will be diminished; the chiefdoms will end; the small and seasonless maguey will accidentally be cut, small immature trees will bear fruit, and the defective earth will be continually diminished.

Then malice, transgressions, and sensuality will reach a height, young boys and girls will have sexual relations, people will rob each others' homes.

Awesome events will occur in this time; the birds will speak and the tree of light, of health and sustenance, will arrive.

To free our children from these vices and calamities, make sure that from an early age they give themselves to integrity and work (Alva Ixtlilxochitl, II, Chap. XLVII).

Quetzalcoatl-Topiltzin, the Toltec chieftain-priest of the Plumed Serpent.
Diego Durán, Historia de las Indias de Nueva España y islas de tierra firme, and Atlas.

Directly facing Huitzilopochtli's temple, Hungry Coyote built an opposing pyramid. On its top he placed a tower nine stories high, one for each of the nine heavens; on the ninth story he put a chapel filled with musical instruments, drums, shells, horns, flutes, bells, cymbals, and then a tenth story with a black roof gilded with stars on the outside and gold, gems, and precious feathers within. This temple, which the people called the Chililitli after one of the instruments, he dedicated to Tloque Nahuaque, the Lord of the With and the By, the Unknown God, Creator of All Things, God of Causes, Master of the Far and the Near, He Who Invented Himself, Life Giver, Who Is as Night and as the Wind. No image was allowed in this temple, only flowers and incense, and no sacrifice of blood. Every day at dawn, noon, sunset, and midnight, the hours at which the sovereign prayed, the instruments would be played to call the people to higher consciousness.

Nahua musicians. Huehuetl, teponaztli, and rattles. Sahagún, Florentine codex.

In recognition of his accomplishments as a visionary, the people began to address him as *tlamatini*, "he who knows," the highest honor that could be paid to a poet in ancient Mexico.

Meanwhile, Azcalxochitzin was approaching the end of her childbearing years and Hungry Coyote himself was aging, but still had no heir. He retired to his hilltop garden retreat at Texcotzingo, where he had built rock-cut baths, sculptures, and a massive aqueduct system. There he fasted forty days. Every day at dawn, midday, sunset, and midnight he prayed and offered copal incense. There he composed sixty songs of praise to the Unknown God, the creator and principle of all things. When he emerged from his retreat, he received news that Azcalxochitzin was pregnant. She bore him a son, Nezahualpilli, "Hungry Prince," who was destined to become a poet almost as renowned as his father.

Nezahualcoyotl's health and vigor remained extraordinary until he reached seventy-one, after reigning forty-two years. Falling ill and realizing his approaching death, he called his children together and named Nezahaulpilli, seven years old, as his successor. "I find myself very close to death," he said, according to Fernando de Alva Ixtlilxochitl, his descendant and biographer, "and when I am dead, instead of sad lamentations, sing happy songs, showing valor and strength in your spirits. . . ."

Hungry Coyote died quietly in his bed in the year 1472, 6 Flint.

The Songs of Dzitbalche

Ancient Mayan Poetry

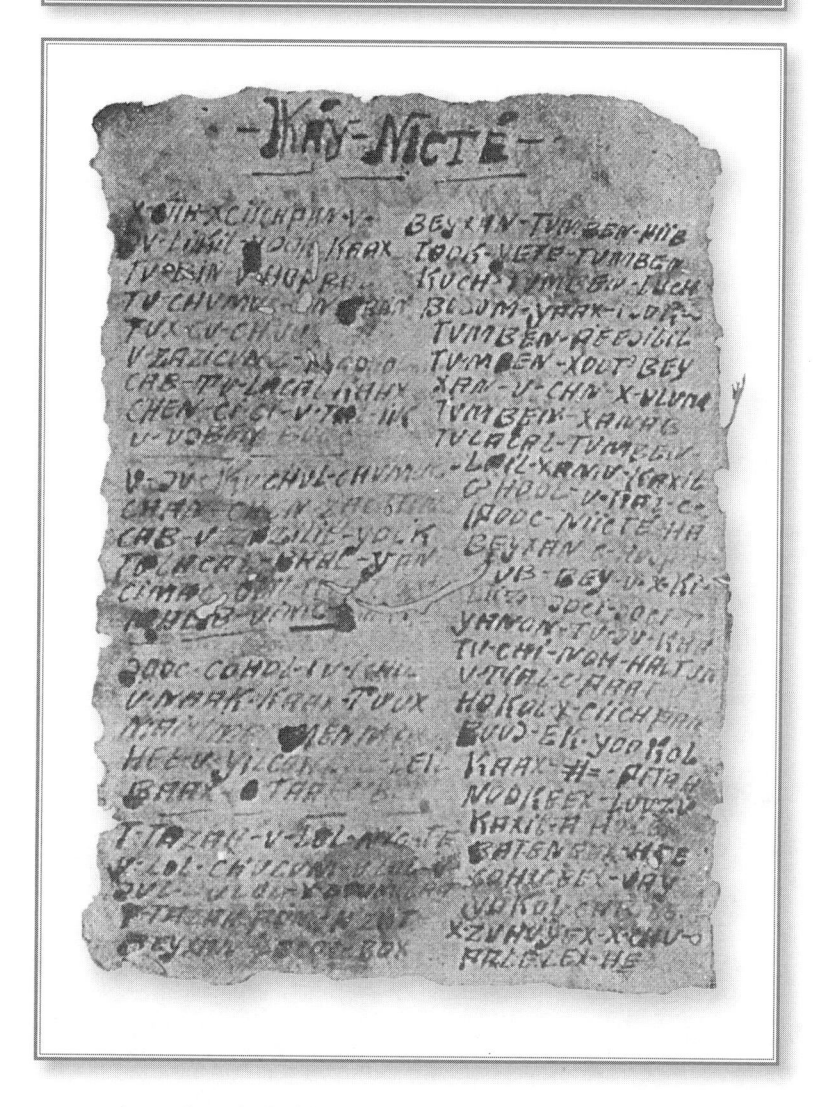

A page from the Dzitbalche manuscript: Kay Nicte/Flower Song.

Introduction

The Songs of Dzitbalche

The Life of Ah Bam

INTRODUCTION

The Songs of Dzitbalche include most of the ancient Maya lyric poetry that has survived. In these songs, the poet speaks of personal feelings and ideas of love, philosophy, ancient rituals, and spiritual values.

The original title page reads, "The Book of the Dances of the Ancients that it was the custom to perform here in the towns when the whites had not yet arrived." The title "Songs of Dzitbalche" was given to the collection by the first translator into Spanish, Alfredo Barrera Vásquez, and it is by this name that it is generally known. Written above the title is the word *kolomche*—a ceremonial dance—and below it is the first poem, "I Will Kiss Your Mouth."

The manuscript itself was probably written in the eighteenth century, though it could be a copy of an earlier manuscript. Some of the material it contains is obviously much older, probably from the fifteenth century. A number of the poems incorporate fragments of ancient ceremonies; others are descriptions of those ceremonies. It is not always possible to distinguish between the two. The poems about the ceremonies were written by Ah Bam during the colonial period, while the ceremonies described are clearly ancient.

Many of the songs begin with an expository section explaining the ceremony related to the song. Most of the poems use the most typical device of Mayan poetry: couplets, the repeating of key words and phrases in consecutive lines. There are, however, very few choruses or refrains.

Four of the pieces could be classified as love (and ritual love) songs: I Will Kiss Your Mouth; Let Us Go to the Receiving of the Flower; Flower Song; and To Kiss Your Lips Beside the Fence Rails.

Two are prayers: To the Great Lord Ah Kulel; The Mourning Song of the Poor Motherless Orphan.

One is a hymn to sunrise: For the Traveler on the Road at Dawn.

At least four of the "songs" appear to have been spoken or chanted like poems. As Barrera Vásquez states, "Although we give the title of songs to all the texts of the codex, some of these appear to be more narrations or explications without any characteristic (of song) other than that of being written in columns, in the manner of meter, without having it properly" (*El libro* 27; my translation).

I have translated fourteen of the songs for this volume.

Mayan songs and dances were of course accompanied by music. An ensemble consisted of flutes, trumpets, whistles, gongs, drums, and rattles. Melodies were played on wooden or reed flutes. The most common Mayan percussion instruments were large horizontal gongs *(tunk'ul'oob)* made from hollowed trees, which were struck with rubber-ended sticks, giving a deep mournful sound; smaller drums made of wood, gourd, or tortoise shell, beaten with the palms; and rattles of clay, wood, or gourd containing seeds or pebbles. There were two kinds of trumpets, one made from a conch shell, the other from a long, thin, hollow stick with a large twisted gourd at its end. Whistles were made from both cane and deer bone.

The Songs of Dzitbalche is closely related to the *Books of Chilam Balam* (the jaguar priest), the "bible" of the Yucatec Mayas. The various existing manuscripts of Chilam Balam also date from the 1700s, but are copies of much earlier material. The name Bam is most likely a contraction of Balam, which means "jaguar."

Beyond the facts that he has included in this manuscript, nothing specific is known about Ah Bam's life. However, much about him can be gathered from the wealth of information known about the time and place.

The Manuscript

The manuscript of the Songs of Dzitbalche surfaced in Mérida, Yucatan, in 1942 as eighteen pages of Spanish paper about 6" x 8-1/2", bound on one side with henequen thread. It was written in colonial Yucatec Maya, with all capital letters, in ink, using a sharpened stick and a feather quill, in the alphabetic script that the Mayas learned during the early colonial period after they were forbidden under penalty of death to write in hieroglyphics or possess screenfold books. The format and layout of the manuscript have similarities to European poetry books. The lyrics or poems are laid out with lines and stanzas, some in two columns. Each song begins on a new page and most have titles. According to the analysis of the extraordinary linguist Barrera Vásquez, the manuscript had to have been made around or after 1742 because certain orthography it uses did not come into practice until then. However, as Barrera Vásquez had to admit, it could easily be a copy of an earlier codex, as was the custom.

Deities

Many of the songs relate to specific Mayan deities, ceremonies, and rituals.

The Mayas had two primary deities, male and female, with many aspects. It is through the different names of their various aspects that they are called on in the Songs.

Itzamna (Iguana House) was the male creator of the universe, the sky deity, the sun. He went by different names according to his many aspects. Among these aspects mentioned in the Songs are Hunabku (One Being God), Kinich Ahau (Father Sun), Cit Bolon Tun (Deity of Medicine) and Kukulcan (Feathered Serpent).

Ix Chel (Rainbow Woman) was the female force, the Creation Goddess, wife of Itzamna. Also known by Ix Chebel Yax and many other names, she was the moon, earth, and bodies of water, and patroness of weaving, painting, procreation, and medicine.

Other important supernatural beings include the deities of rain (*Chac'oob*), of maize, of the planet Venus, the four *Bacab* who each held up a corner of the world, and the gods of evil, death, and the underworld (*Metnal* or *Xibalba*).

Ceremonies in the Songs
Receiving of the Flower

Song: Let Us Go To The Receiving of the Flower.

The Receiving of the Flower was the wedding ceremony. In this song it seems to be a public ceremony in the town center, though other sources place it in the bride's house.

Itzamna, the sky god, and Ix Chel, the moon goddess. Itzamna is from Morley, The Ancient Maya.
Ix Chel is from Anonymous, Cholb'al Q'ij Agenda Maya.

FLOWER CEREMONY

Song: Flower Song.

The Flower Ceremony was a rite to keep or bring back a lover. A group of women, under the direction of a female elder, met at night at a rock spring in the woods by the light of the moon. While the group of naked singers danced around her, the patient, also naked, threw plumeria flowers into the water, transforming it into a love potion.

INTERROGATION OF THE CHIEFS CEREMONY

Song: Lord Rattlesnake, Lord Precious Feathered Serpent

The purpose of the interrogation of the chiefs in the language of Zuyua was to ascertain the lineage credentials of Mayan chiefs. The interrogator was the *halach uinic*, the "true man," the *batab*. The ritual took place at the beginning of each new *katun*. It consisted of a series of arcane questions in an occult language based on Toltec-Itza knowledge, with the equally arcane answers known only to those in families eligible to

INTRODUCTION/THE SONGS OF DZITBALCHE   *59*

become chiefs. The questions and answers had supposedly been passed down from father to son since the fall of Tula, the city in central Mexico where Kukulcan was ruler before he and his followers emigrated to Yucatan.

This poem tells a mythological story in verse, a tale similar to the Egyptian story of the sphinx. Kukulcan (Quetzalcoatl, Feathered Serpent), named only in the title, is the protagonist who answers the riddle and thus defeats the centipede. Kukulcan represents enlightenment in the struggle with the forces of darkness. This myth probably refers to the ceremony of the interrogation of the chiefs. In another interpretation, Edmonson suggests that the centipede and the seven jumping heads represent the Spaniards and their seven-day week.

Calendar Ceremonies

Songs: The Dark Days of the Last Month of the Year; Those Who Build Houses and Temples; Speech to the Lord, Sustainer of the Tun-Years; Speech of Cit Bolon, Priest of the Tun Year, Savant of the Uinal Month; Extinguishing the Ancient One on the Mountain.

In one way or another all Mayan ceremonies are calendrical. Mayan culture is so infused with calendar lore that it is difficult to understand the culture without studying the calendar as well.

Counting days was the basis for all Maya calendrics. They kept track of two basic cycles upon which all the others were built: the Sacred Year of 260 days and the solar year of 365 days.

There were 20 different days (*kin'oob*). The 260-day sacred year was formed by combining the 20 days with the numbers 1 to 13. The Maya solar year (*haab*) was divided into 18 months (*uinal'oob*) of 20 days, which made a 360-day *tun*, plus a final month of five days, the *uayeb*, adding up to 365 days.

The last two uinal months before the end of the year stressed pleasures and diversions. However, the five-day *uayeb* was dangerous and unlucky, a period of abstention from food, washing, and sex. If the *uayeb* ceremonies were not conducted properly, a year of sickness and disaster might result. A *uayeb* would someday lead to the end of this world. There were four different year-bearers, deities who presided over years in rotation.

For the *uayeb* (referred to in "The Dark Days of the Last Month of the Year"), an idol of one of the patron deities was set up at the house of one of the principal chiefs. Another idol was erected at a pile of stones at one of the four cardinal points outside of town, and a special road was built to it with arches of green branches. There they made offerings to the deity, then carried the idol to the house of the chief, where the ceremonies continued. The new year was a time of renewal. All utensils were destroyed and new ones made. The "Ancient One" referred to in "Extinguishing the Ancient One on the Mountain" was the temple ("mountain") fire, which was extinguished after having been kept burning all year, after which "new fire" was kindled with a fire drill.

The *katun* was a 7,200-day cycle (almost 20 years) made of 20 tuns (360 days). There were 13 different *katun'oob*, each with different auguries and predictable tendencies. In this way they saw history as repeating. This was the basic time frame in which the Mayas recorded their history. They kept track of what happened in each *katun* so as to better deal with the present and future. A commemorative stone was erected at the end of each *katun*. The ending of one *katun* and the beginning of a new one was also probably the occasion of a *kolomche* dance, the subject of two poems in the original Dzitbalche anthology, but not translated in this current selection. The *kolomche* was a cultural transformation of the arrow ceremony, in which a high-ranking captive was ritually shot. In the dance, one dancer would throw arrowlike reeds at another, but the would-be target would catch them all and triumph, cheating death. Similarly, the ending of each *katun* did not signal doom, but a new beginning.

There is far too much information about the Maya calendar and its ceremonies to cover here. I encourage the reader to pursue this knowledge, which can be obtained from many excellent sources.

THE YUCATEC MAYA LANGUAGE

The Mayan language family diverged from a common stock over the centuries into the large variety of related languages found throughout the Maya region today, much as the Romance languages diverged from Latin. There are twenty-eight Mayan languages with numerous dialects. Yucatec Maya, however, forms one of the three major subgroupings, the others being Huastecan and Southern Mayan. All Mayan language speakers together total about four million people. Yucatec Maya remains understandable throughout the Yucatan peninsula, despite minor local differences. Over 450,000 people speak Maya in Yucatan today.

Mayan word roots are often strung together to form long compound words, one of which can express an entire English sentence. Nouns with possessive pronouns often replace verbs. Instead of "they eat," a Maya would say, "their eating." The subject usually follows the possessed verb and its object; for example, "the boys ate food" would be translated as "their eat past food the boys." However, word order is flexible, and any word can go first depending on what is being emphasized. Yucatec Maya is glottalized in some consonants, tonal in certain vowels, and uses glottal stops.

SIMPLIFIED GUIDE TO MAYA PRONUNCIATION

Vowels and consonants approximately as in Spanish, except:

c = English /k/

x = English /sh/

dz, tz = English /ts/

u followed by another vowel = English /w/

Glottalized sounds (emphatic versions): The sounds usually written today as p', t', dz' (ts'), ch' and k' do not exist in English or Spanish. They are glottalized or explosive versions of p, t, ts, ch and c made by holding the breath and then releasing it while making the sound. The glottis closes as the tongue reaches the point of articulation for the consonant, then it opens at the same time the letter is pronounced, making a distinctive popping sound.

Colonial Mayan was written in a number of variations. The most common are:

ph, pp = p'
th = t'
dz = ts'
chch = ch'

Yucatec Maya uses tone the way English uses stress. There are three tones: high, neutral, and low, with the voice rising on the last syllable of most words, but sometimes on the penultimate. Aside from this, vowels should always be given full value (never reduced to the schwa as in English) and intonation should be kept as flat and even as possible. Maya can sound somewhat singsong to anglophones.

LINGUISTIC GUIDE TO MAYA PRONUNCIATION

	phoneme	*modern variants*	*colonial alphabets*	*colonial variants*
vowels	/ā/, /ä/, /a/		a	
	/ē/, /e/		e	
	/i/		i	
	/o/		o	
	/ü/, /u/		u	
consonants	/b/		b	
	/ch/	c	ch	
	/ch'/	c'	ch'	chh, chch, ch
	/h/	j	h	
	/k/		c	
	/k'/		k	
	/l/		l	
	/m/		m	
	/n/		n	
	/p/		p	
	/p'/		p'	pp, p
	/s/		s	z, ç
	/sh/	s, sh	x	
	/t/		t	
	/t'/		t'	tt, th, t
	/ts/	tz	tz	
	/ts'/	dz, tz'	dz	o
	/w/		u	
	/y/		y	

The Songs of Dzitbalche

An almanac page from the Madrid codex. At the lower right is a scribe. Deities play drums and rattles: the rain god Chac (upper and lower left); the corn god (top and center right); the sky god Itzamna (center left), inventor of books and writing, and associated with Kukulkan, the feathered serpent. The vulture signifies rain of little value.

(1)

BIN IN TZ'UUTZ' A CHI'

Bin in tz'uutz' a chi'
tut yam x cohl.
X ciichpam zac,
yan yan a uahal.

(1)

I WILL KISS YOUR MOUTH

I will kiss your mouth
between the plants of the milpa.
Shimmering beauty,
you have to awake.

(2)

TZ'UTZ' A CHI
T U CAAP COOL HOK CHE

Tz'aex a hatz'uutz nokeex;
tz'ooc u kuchul kin h'cimac olil;
xeech u tzou tzotzel a pol;
tz'a u lemceech ciichcelmil a nok
tz'a hatz'utz xanaab;
ch'uuycinzah a nuucuuch tuup
tu tupil a xicin;
tz'a malob oochh';
tz'a u keexiloob a x ciichpan caal;
tz'a, uu baakaal
hop men hop tu nak a kab.
T kailbeilt caa i laac ciichpameech
hebiix [maix] maace
uay tu t cahil,
H' Tz'iitbalchee' cah.

In yacumaech
X Cichpan Colelbiil.
Lai beiltic
in kaat ca i[labe]ech
h'aach zempeech
cii[chpam]ech,
tumen cu yan
ca chiicpaaceech ti x buutz' ek,
tu men ca u tz'iboolteech
tac lail
u yetel u x lol nicte kaax.

Chen zacan
zacan a nok,
h'x zuhuy,
xen a tz'a u cimac olil a chee
tz'a utz ta puczikal
tumen helae
u zutucil cimac olil
tu lacal uinic
lail cu tz'ailc
u yutzil ti teech.

(2)

TO KISS YOUR LIPS
BESIDE THE FENCE RAILS

Put on your beautiful clothes;
the day of happiness has arrived;
comb the tangles from your hair;
put on your most attractive clothes
and your splendid leather;
hang great pendants in the lobes of
your ears; put on
a good belt; string garlands
around your shapely throat;
put shining coils
on your plump upper arms.
Glorious you will be seen,
for none is more beautiful here
in this town, the seat of Dzitbalche.

I love you, beautiful lady.
I want you to be seen; in
truth you are very alluring,
I compare you to the smoking star
because they desire you up to the moon
and in the flowers of the fields.

Pure and white are your clothes, maiden.
Go give happiness with your laugh,
put goodness in your heart, because today
is the moment of happiness; all people
put their goodness in you.

(3)

COOX H C KAM NIICTE'

Cimaac olailil
tan c kayiic
tumen bin cah
C'Kam C'Niicte.
Tulacailil x chuup x loob bayen
chen chehlah chehlameec u yiich
tut ziit u puucziikalil
tut tz'uu u tzem.
Bail x tumen?
tumen yoheel
t'yolal u tz'iic
u zuhuyil colelil ti u yaa[cunah]

Kayeex Nicteil!

C'yant ceex Naacon
yetel Noh Yum Ah'Kulel
ah tan caan chee.
Ah Culel hkay:
"Coneex coneex
c'tz'a c'olaalil tu taan X Zuhuz
X Ciichpan Zuhuy
Colelbil u Lolil Loob ayen
Tut can caan che
[U] Colebil X M . . . Zuhuy Kaak u,
beyx[a]n x ci[c]h[p]an X'Kamleooch,
X ciichpan X ah Zoot,
yete[l] x ciichpam colel
x zuhuy X Ttoot much.
Laitie tz'iic utzil
cuxtalil uay yo[k] peet[n]e
uay yo[k] chakme
tu zuut lumil uay uitzil."

Coox coox
coneex palaleex:
beey c tz'aic cici cimac
olil uay Tz'itil Piich
Tz'itilbalche.

(3)

LET US GO
TO THE RECEIVING OF THE FLOWER

Let us sing
flowing with joy
because we are going to
the Receiving of the Flower.
All the maidens
wear a smile on their pure faces;
their hearts
jump in their breasts.
What is the cause?
Because they know
that they will give
their virginity to those they love.

Let the Flower sing!

Accompanying you will be the Nacom
and the Great Lord Ah Kulel
present on the platform.
Ah Kulel sings:
"Let us go, let us go
lay down our wills before the virgin,
the beautiful virgin and lady,
the flower of the maidens
on the high platform,
the Lady Suhuy Kaak,
the pretty X'Kamleooch,
the lovely X'Zoot
and the beautiful
lady virgin X'T'oot'much.
They are those who give goodness
to life here in this region,
on the plains and in the district
here in the mountains."

Let us go, let us go,
let us go, youths;
we will give perfect rejoicing
here in Dzitill Piich,
Dzitbalche.

(4)

KAY NICTE'

X ciih x ciichpan u
tz' u likil yook kaax;
tu bin u hopbal
tu chumuc c[a]n [c]aan
tux cu ch'uuytal u zazicunz
yookol cab tu lacal kaax
chen cici u tal iik u utz'ben booc.
U tz' u kuchul
chumuc caan
chen zacttin cab u zazilil
yook tulacal baal.
Yan cimac olil ti u tulacal malob uinic.

Tz'ooc cohol tu ichil u naak kaax
tuux maixi mac men max
hel u yilconeil leil
baax [c] taal c'beet.

T tazah u lol nicte',
u lol chucum, u lol u tz'tul,
u lol x . . . milah;
t tazah pom,
h'ziit,
beyxan x coc box,
beyxan tumben hiib took yete tumben
kuch tumben luch,
bolom yaax took,
tumben peetz'ilil,
tumben xoot,
beyxan u can x ulum tumben xanab,
tu lacal tumben lail xam u kaxil c'hool,
u tial c pooc niicte' ha
beyxan c hoopza
[h] ub bey u x kiliiz.

(4)

FLOWER SONG

The most alluring moon
has risen over the forest;
it is going to burn
suspended in the center
of the sky to lighten
all the earth, all the woods,
shining its light on all.
Sweetly comes the air and the perfume.
It has arrived in the middle
of the sky,
glowing radiance
over all things.
Happiness permeates all good men.

We have arrived inside the woods
where no one will see
what we have
come here to do.

We have brought plumeria flowers,
chucum blossoms, dog jasmine,
milah blooms;
we have the copal,
the low cane vine,
the land tortoise shell,
new quartz, hard chalk powder
and new cotton thread,
the new gourd cup,
the large fine flint,
the new weight,
the new needle work,
gifts of turkeys, new leather,
all new, even our hair bands,
they touch us with nectar
of the roaring conch shell
of the ancients.

Tz'oci, tz'oci
t yan on tu tz'u kaa[x],
tu chi noh haltun
utial c'paat u hokol
x ciichpan buutz' ek
yookol kaax.
Pitah nookeex
luuz u kaxil a holex
ba teneex
hee cohiceex uay yokol cabile
x zuhuyex x chupalelex hel u.

Already, already
we are in the heart of the woods,
at the edge of the pool in the stone
to await the rising
of the lovely smoking star
over the forest.
Take off your clothes,
let down your hair,
become as you were
when you arrived here on earth,
virgins, maidens.

(5)

U YAYAH KAY
H'OTZIL X MA NA
X PAM OKOOT CHE

Hach chiichanen caa cim in na
caa cim in yum.
Ay ay in Yumen!
Caa t ppaten tu kab
t yicnal in laak
miix maac yanten uay yokol cab.
Ay ay in yumilen!
Cu man cappel kin
cu cimil ten in laak
tin ttuluch c' ppat cen
tin ttuluch hum. Ay ay!

Tz'u man lail kin tin hun ppat cen
caa tu han ch'ahen u bizen t nin
u ppel tz'ul tu kab.
Ay ay in yumilen!
H'loobil hach yaab yayab loob
tin manziic uay
yokol ca[b]. Miix ua bikin
bin hauc in uokol.

Miix in uonel yan
hach chen tin hum
chen bey in man
uay tin lum
h'kin yetel akab
chen okol okol
xuupzic in uich
lail xuupziic ool.
Yam loob hach chich.
Ay in Yum!
Ch'aten otzilil tz'a u tibitil
leil yah muukyaa.
Tz'aten u tz'oc cimilil
ua tz'aten toh olal
in Ciichcelem Yumil!

(5)

THE MOURNING SONG
OF THE POOR MOTHERLESS ORPHAN
DANCE TO DRUMBEATS

I was very small when my mother died,
when my father died.
Ay ay, my Lord!
Left in the hands
and company of friends,
I have no family here on earth.
Ay ay, my Lord!
Two days ago my friends died,
and left me insecure
vulnerable, alone. *Ay ay*!

That day I was alone
and put myself
in a stranger's hand.
Ay ay, my lord!
Evil, much evil
passes here
on earth. Perhaps
I will never stop crying.

Without family,
alone,
very lonely I walk
here in my land,
crying day and night
only cries consume my eyes and soul.
Under evil so hard.
Ay, my Lord!
Take pity on me, put an end
to this suffering.
Give me death,
or give my soul transcendence
my beautiful Lord!

Otzil otzil co . . .
baai tu hun yook lum
ua yan ca u kaat
tu ttuluch hum
kaat men kaat tu hol nah nahil
tu lacal maac ilic
heleili u tz'iic yacunail.
Inan yotoch inam u nok
inan kaak.
Ay in Yum! Chaten otzilil!
Tz'ate[n] toholal utial caa paatac
in muuk yahtic.

Poor, poor
alone on earth
pleading
insecure lonely
imploring door to door
asking every person I see to give me love.
I who have no home, no clothes,
no fire.
Ay my Lord! Have pity on me!
Give my soul transcendence
to endure.

(6)

H'KAY BALTZ'AM

Kin kuilancail t cah nahlil.
U caa'h htippil t'zazilil kin tut haal caan
t cu bin u bin bey no[hol]
bai t x[aman] bey t la[kin] bey xan t chi[kin],
tumtal u zazil yokol cabilil
eh hook c'hen tiul tz'iic . . .
X kuuluuch yeet maaz yeet chiic
h'k . . . [yeet] x tz'unun
cu yaalcab t cuchil.

X baach, x zac pacal, tz'uutz'uuz,
bey nom, chaan beech, yeet x kook, x zac chich,
calicil h'zaay c'yalcu . . . ben
lail kaxil chiich cu hoopz cu kay tumen
h'eeb ziamcen utzilil.

X Ciichpan Ek
hohopnan yook kaax
cu butz'ilan ca lamat lamat
u taal u cimil u
yook yaxil kaax.

Cimmaac olilil kin kuilail uay
tee t cahalil;
tumen tumben kin c'tal zaztal
t tulacal uinicil t cah muulba uay
t cahalil.

(6)

THE SONG OF THE MINSTREL

Today the divine fiesta begins in the villages.
Dawn streams over the horizon,
south, north, east, west,
light comes to the earth,
darkness is gone.
Roaches, crickets, fleas, and moths
hurry home.

Magpies, white doves, swallows,
partridges, mockingbirds, thrushes, quail,
red ants rush about,
all the forest birds begin their songs because
morning dew brings happiness.

The beautiful star
shines over the woods,
smoking as it sinks and vanishes;
the moon too dies
over the forest green.

Happiness of fiesta day has arrived
here in the village;
a new sun brings light
to all who live together here
in the village.

(7)

HTI TU BELIL UA UTAAL KIN UAY

Tii ca kay, chan zac pacal
tu kablail yaa[x] che.
Tii yan xan x ciip chohil chan x chuuleeb
beyxan x kukun lail zac chich
tu lacal ciimac yool
u yalaakoob Yum Ku.

Hebix xan H'Colebil yan yaalak h'e . . .
ix chan x muukuy, chan x tz'itz'iibil
Yetel xan x chinchinbaclal
lail xan x tz'unuun.
lail laiix u yaalak chiich'
X Ciichpan Xunan Colebil.

Lail ua yan cimaac [olil] ichil lay bal cheob
baax ten ma u cimaactal ol ton?
Ua beiloob laitiob tac tu zaztal
pencech hatz'utzoob
chen kay chen baxaal
cu man tu tucuuloob.

(7)

FOR THE TRAVELER ON THE ROAD AT DAWN

Doves singing
in the ceiba branches there,
flycatchers, little yellow birds,
cuckoos, mockingbirds there,
all happy,
the birds of the Lord.

Likewise the lady has her birds:
the little birds, the small cardinals,
canaries, hummingbirds,
they are the birds of the beautiful lady.

If such happiness is among the animals,
why shouldn't our hearts be happy too?
At dawn they are
most beautiful
when only songs and games
pass in their thoughts.

(8)

T NOHHOCH YUM AH CULEL T'CAHIL TZ'ITBALCHE', AHHAU CAN PE[C]H

Talen talen
tut taan a caan chei
in nahmaat teech
a cici olal H'Ciichcelem In Yum,
tut men teech
ca tz'ic u malobil
utzil baal yanal a ka[b],
yan a uutzil
lohil than.

Ten cin uilic baax uutz
yet baxil kaaz uay
t tee lumail tz'aten a zazil,
in Hahal Yum,
tz'aaten yaab naatil
tinih tucul yeettel ti in naat,
utial caa in chinchin hool teech
zamat zamat kin.

Likiic u puul yahil
Tu uey cizin ti uokol
Ua ma hah baax
cin tzeectic techi
Cimic in na, cimic in yum,
Cimic in co[lel], cimic in ualaak
Ua bax cin tzolic inYum
Cin ba . . .

Haah ten cin ka[tic i t]eech,
Ciichcelem Yumil Can,
nohoc[h] cheech ta cuchil
t caanil ley cin ttziiceech
Ciichc[elem] T Humnaab Ku . . .
teech ca tz'iic uu[tzil]
beyilil kazil b[aal] uay yokol cabe
ten ttanilcee[ch] t Nohhoch Yum,
Ah Culel.

(8)

TO THE GREAT LORD AH KULEL OF THE TOWN OF DZITBALCHE, AND HIGH PRIEST PECH

I have come, come
before your lofty tree,
my beautiful Lord,
to ask happiness,
because you bestow no evil,
only good is in your hand,
I ask your blessing,
your redeeming words.

I see good and evil
in this land,
so shine your light on me,
true Father,
plant understanding into my thoughts
and into my intelligence,
so I can honor you every day.

If what I declare is not true,
hurl harmful spells
of the demon witch at me,
let my mother die, let my father die,
my wife, my animals, let them all die,
if what I say, my Father,
is not true.

I implore you,
Beautiful Sky Father,
great in your seat above,
I revere you,
beautiful and only Lord,
you who dispense good
and bad here on earth,
I call on you, Great Father,
Governor.

(9)

KAMA THAN TIH
U YUM LATT KAB TUNOOB

In yumileex cin taal cheen
chinchin u taaniil in uich.
Tz'ooc kin bolon
ma in tunt mix ilmail x chupil,
mix in chau cohol
ah kaz tuculil tin nattil.
otzil tumen
cin taal yeetel in tum[b]en uitt
in tumben piixen tzemilil.
yeetal xan yan cah uile, in Yum,
ten ma' ti caaxtiic u kazil
keban tu tan a uich
in hahal Yum Humnab K[u],
laibetic chen
t zaac han zaac in pixam
in tal in u[i]leech ta cuchil
tumen ti teech cin k[u]bic
tu tuliz
in uolal yetel in tuc[u]l
uay yokol lumeil.

T cheen teech ci alah uoltic
uay tee yokol cabil.
tumen teech, Nohochil Kin,
ca tz'ic u[t]z uay
yokol cab ti tulacal baal
yan u cuuxtal
tumen teec[h] tz'anneech a
laattleil lum
tuux cu cuxt[al] tu lacal uin[ic]
yetel teech u ha lohill
ca tz'iic utzilil.

(9)

SPEECH TO THE LORD, SUSTAINER OF THE TUN-YEARS

My fathers, I come
with my face bowed.
Nine days
I have not touched or visited a woman,
nor permitted evil thoughts
to enter my mind.
I am poor
yet I come with new trousers,
new tunic.
And thus, my Father, as you will see,
I am not looking for evil in my heart
as I come before your face,
my true one God father,
but for purity,
my soul like dawn,
I come to see you in your place,
to bring you
my entire will and consciousness
here on Earth.

Only in you
do I confide entirely
in this world,
because you, O great sun,
grant goodness
here on earth
to all things alive,
because you are the giver
and sustainer of this earth
where all people live,
you are the true redeemer
who gives only good.

(10)

H'UAYAH YAAB
T'KAAL
KIN EEK

U kinil t'okol u kinil
kaziil baal. Chakaab cizin
hekaab miitnal,
in nan utzil chen yan lobil
a huat yetel okol.
Tz'ooc u man hun ppel tuliz haab
lail habil h'kaban h'elae.

Cutaibal xan hun kal
kin x ma kaba
u yail kin u kinil loob
h eek kinoob.

Inan x ciichpan zazilil t yiich
H'unaab Ku u tial u palil
uay yok[ol] cab,
tumen ti lei kin kinooba
tum ppizil u keban yokol cab
tu lacal uinic:
xiib yetel x chuup
chi[ch]an yetel nohoch
otzil yetel ayikal, miatz yetel h'num
Ah'haucan, Aculel
Batab, Nacon, Chacoob
Chumthanoob, Tupiloob.
Tulacal uinic hellae cu ppizil u keban
tiail lail kin; tumen bin kuuchoc
u kinil lai
tiel kina u tz'ooc yokol cab.

(10)

THE DARK DAYS OF THE LAST MONTH OF THE YEAR

The days of crying, the days
of evil. The demon is free,
the infernos open,
there is no goodness, only evil,
laments and cries.
An entire year has passed,
the year numbered here.

Come is a month of
days without name,
painful days, days of evil,
black days.

The beautiful light of the eyes of
Hunabku for his earthly sons
has not yet come,
because during these days
the transgressions of all people on earth
are measured:
men and women, children and adults
poor and rich, wise and ignorant;
Lord Serpent, commissioner,
governor, captain, rain priest,
councilors, constables.
All people's transgressions are measured in
these days; because the time
will come when
these days will mark the end
of the world.

Tum[e]m
tu bizic u xocxocil tu lacal
u kkeban uincoob
u uay t lume tumen.
Ti u tz'ic hun ppeel
x nuc homa
betan yetel u kaat h'kamaz tu lacal
u yalil yich lei
max cu yok ticoo lob
cu mental tiob
uay t lum.
Lai can h'tulnaac lail x nuc homaa
cu tz'o.

For this
there will be a count of all
the transgressions of people
here on earth.
Into a great glass
made from the clay of tree termites,
Hunabku puts the tears
from those who cry over the evils
done on earth.
When the great glass is filled to the brim
it will end.

(11)

HUA PAACH'OOB YETEL PPUZ[OOB]

Tz'u lam kaa[bet]
u ppizil u xociil ua hayppel haab ua katum
kin maan[aac]
le u kinil uay te cahobaa leil
h nucuuch chaac uincoob
laitiob liiz u pa[ak] leil
u uchben cahob
helah c'ilic
uay Peten H'Chakan,
tu lacal lail cahoob ttittanoob
yook lum
uay helah
taan c'ilic ttuuch
men ttuuch yokol canal uitzoob.

Lail cu talziic
tu uay t cahoob c tz'iic
u thanilbaal [baal] lail c'iliic hela
baax c ohelma;
tumen zazammal
ci ilic t c chumuuc caan
u chiculil bax alan ton
tumen h uuchben uincoob
uay t cahale,
uay t lume.

Ti c tz'iic u hahil c ool
u tial caa paactac
xocic u ba[al] yan t yiich
lai caan yo[co]l akab bay tu c chum
tu chumu[c] beyua tun chimil
tan canza.

(11)

THOSE WHO BUILD HOUSES AND TEMPLES

Essential
to count the haab years or katun'oob
that have passed since
the great powerful men
raised the walls of the ancient cities
that we see now
here in the province of the plains,
all these cities scattered
on the earth
here and there, on high hills.

Here in the cities, we try to give
meaning to what we see today in the skies
and what we know;
for day to day
at midday
we see in the skies
the signs told to us by
the ancient people of this land,
the ancient people of these villages
here on our earth.

Let us purify our hearts
so at nightfall,
and at midnight,
from horizon to zenith
we may read the face of the sky.

(12)

AH'TZAAB CAN
H KUUKUL KUUL CAN

Ti teech
uinic
tal in uailic
baaxten uay peten,
uay h chakan,
uay te lum
c u [uc]hben huapaach uincoob
hebiix xan h ppuuz
maliicil cohoc teil
lumoob maix
maic x uinic bayanon
tz'ooc u yantaal
lemceech yaab kin
uay cu ximbanccuba
Xah Chaapaat
hum uuc u tiichil u pol yaat chen
laiti ca uilic
u kaatal ta beel
utial u hanteech
yetel u tial u tz'a teech
loobil tah cuxtal
ua ma ta naatiic
baax cu kaatic teich.

Ma tun hel caa kuuch u kinil
u yantaahma maix l u ailic
tie ca tu yuub, he caah
tz'iicinahi
tumen laitiel
maix u . . . chahal u tz'iic
leil u nuctah tiel
Ah X Chapaat laiti nuce tii.

Laibetiic haach tu chah lobil
le baax cu tz'iic u yaal
nucatiel tumen h'tabz[a]biel tumen.

(12)

LORD RATTLESNAKE
LORD PRECIOUS FEATHERED SERPENT

To you,
human,
I come to tell you
that here in this region,
this plain,
here in this land,
back in the era of ancient giants
and hunchbacks
when even no people such as us
had as yet ever arrived,
a very long time ago
Lord Centipede passed here,
and had with him seven jumping heads;
you could see them
quickly crossing the road
to devour you
or put evil
in your life
if you could not understand
the riddle he asked.

But the day arrived
when there was one who answered.
When he heard,
Lord Centipede became furious
because one had understood, responded
and answered his riddle.

So it was Lord Centipede
who was the one who was tricked,
became gravely ill, and died.

(13)

KIILIIZ TUUP
YOK UITZ

Kaman kin tu haal caan
t chikin
tunkul h' huub yetel zacatán
tii t h'hoopz x kay luuch
xiix tun tulacal [pax] tut tazahal oc.

X ppiitum cu bin u kuuchul
tu tanleil Popil Nah Yum Ahau Can
ti an xan H'Holpoop
yetel H'Ch'aacoob
bey Yum Ah Culel yetel u amtahatz'aob.
Tz'u kuchul h'pax kayoob
hpaal tz'amoob h'okotoob h'ualak
zutz'iithoob bey h'ppuuz
yetel nac yaob.
Tu lacal u uinicil . . . tal tu pach
Ah'Ahau Can
tu cimac olil cu beetabil
tu ch[u]muc kiuicil leil c cahtalil.

Tz'u h'ooppol yoocol kin
tu h'aal na caan,
tu tiibit [ta]al u hooppol
lail x . . . pom . . .
Yum Caan kamiic
u buutz' kak utial u chiil
t cu yiich Yum Kin.

Coneex
coon t chum yaax che'
coox tz'aic c keex
u tial tumben haab.
Tz'ooc tz'oocil u maan yaayaa kinil
cooneex u muulail tambalil cahalil,
coni lakin
u tz'ay u xocomcheil
Kiliiz Kaam Kak
yookol uitz.

(13)

EXTINGUISHING THE ANCIENT ONE ON THE MOUNTAIN

The sun sinks into the lap
of the western sky,
the drum beats, the conch trumpets,
the singing gourds sound,
all people assemble.

The acrobats leap as they arrive
at the Council House of Lord Serpent,
where the Chief Holpop
and the Rain Priests wait,
along with Lord Ah Kulel and his attendants.
The minstrels have arrived, the
clowns, dancers, contortionists,
jumpers, hunchbacks,
and spectators.
All the people have come to see
Lord Serpent
and delight at
the performance in the plaza.

As the sun sinks
into the lap of the sky,
it is the moment to begin.
Light the copal.
Lord Sky receives
the smoke and fire
for the face of Father Sun.

Then let us go,
go to the trunk of the ceiba tree
to make our offerings
for the new year.
The painful days are gone,
we will reunite in the village.
We go to the east of the village,
to the wooden column of the ancestor,
the Receiver of the Fire
on the mountaintop.

Taal zeeix l tu lacal baal tumben;
puleex tu lacal baal h'uuchben.

Yum Ku tz'u tz'iic cah
c manz u lobil kin
uay t cahalil
tumen u cah tal u laik kin,
u laik uinal,
u laik haab,
u laik kaatum.

Utial u tal u chucpahal un kaal haab
utial h'katum,
cooneex
c tz'ailc
tumben xuul tum
tu hol cah'nalil.
C caaxtic h'zac tuniich
utial c eeziic
u laak haab u man . . .

Bring all new things;
throw away all the old.

Lord God has granted
that the evil days,
the last days of the year,
which we have passed
together here in the village,
the evil days have ended,
and another day has come,
another uinal month,
another haab year,
another twenty-year katun.

To complete
the count of years for the katun,
we will erect a new stone
to mark its end
at the village gate.
We will find
a white stone
and mark the passing
of another year.

(14)

PAAY CHI'
H'ZIIT H'BOLOM T[U]M
UINALTE' H'MIATZ

Uinalte' paay chi'
H'miatz tz'ac yah
Ti u yan pomol chi kaax
Beec kaaxin
Tikal tikal o hom.
Ch'iic lum paak
Bacalche, h'bohom
Bey [li]kin bey xaman
Bey [chi]kin bey noh'hol
Ti cu taal tu camppel xaay
Beil can
Tuux yan u popil
Nahil bel h'miatz
Hunnaab Ku i
Laiil cu kaazic ti uinic
Tahl han cuuxtal
Uay yokol [ca]b
Ti maax ac u kaat u tz'a u baa . . .
Yol h'cambal.

U uay t'lumil [y]an
U tz'iic tu toh yolal
H'tumen u Yumil
Kaak ha iik lum
Yumil uay yokol cab
Tut tu lah c bail mentahan,
Tumen Yum Hunnaab Ku,
Lait liti
Tz'iic utz yeet kaaz ichil
Maloob yetellob
Tu men lait tie
Cu tz'iic u zazilil yokol cab
Tumen laiti u yumil

AH BAM

(14)

SPEECH OF CIT BOLON
PRIEST OF THE TUN YEAR
SAVANT OF THE UINAL MONTH

The Curer Sage
speaks to open each month,
so medicinal herbs can be found in the woods,
borage in the woods,
in rolls in rolls
he takes the living herbs,
borage, heliotrope,
from the east as from the north,
from the west as from the south,
he comes by the four branches
of the road of the skies
to the mat,
to the house of the wise,
of Hunabku, the only God,
who reminds us
that life here is difficult in this world
for whoever wants
to put himself in the fires
of comprehension.

He gives health
here on earth,
the lord
of fire, water, air, soil,
lord of the world,
of all things
made by him,
Lord Hunabku,
he who distributes
the good and the bad
to good and bad people,
he who gives light to earth,
because he is the father,

Tu lacal baal yan
Yan lu kab,
Bey kin bey h'u
Bey x buutz' ek,
Be u lol zaz caan
Bey muyal bey chaac
Bey h x lelem bey
H'uz bey ch'iich
Bey baal che
Bey.

the keeper of all things,
all things under his hand,
thus sun and moon
thus the smoking star,
that luminous flower
of the skies,
thus clouds and rain,
thus lightning and the smallest fly,
thus creatures of the air and the ground,
thus.

THE LIFE OF AH BAM

The byline of the Songs of Dzitbalche gives us almost all the information we know about the author, Ah Bam, but that is really a wealth of information. It reads, "This book was written by the honorable Mr. Bam, great-grandson of the great Ah Kulel of the town of Dzitbalche in the year 1440." That date cannot refer to the writing, because the only existing manuscript uses the European alphabet and can be reliably dated to some three hundred years later. The manuscript, however, could be a copy or a copy of a copy of a copy, which was standard practice. Much in the contemporary *Books of Chilam Balam* started out in ancient hieroglyphic form, and many of the Songs of Dzitbalche clearly date from long before the Spanish invasion. It is entirely possible that the Songs are a translation of an ancient hieroglyphic book into alphabetic Maya.

However, it is most likely that Ah Bam lived during the colonial period and was a follower of the old culture and a collector of ancient songs. On this assumption, we can reconstruct his life to some degree.

Besides the Maya name Bam, he must have had a Christian name too because he had to have been baptized. But significantly, he chose not to use his Christian name in the manuscript. He was obviously writing for a traditional Mayan audience, not a Spanish one.

He must have been sent to a Franciscan school, where all the children of noble lineages learned to read and write Maya using Spanish characters. Biblical writings and choir songbooks were the main texts. We can see the form of the choir song in the way the Dzitbalche poems are laid out by lines in the European manner.

Alongside the official colonial government, a traditional Mayan government continued, often almost invisible to the conquerors. This shadow government, made up of elders of the lineages, as it had been since ancient times, was the organization that really ran things and held the society together. Ah Bam was clearly a prominent person in that system. He was probably prominent in the colonial system as well, perhaps even the town clerk, whose job it was to transcribe community business in alphabetic Mayan, a position that the Spaniards created in every town in northern Yucatan.

Ah Bam was an elder when he wrote his book. To achieve prominence in Yucatecan Maya society necessitated marriage and a large family, so we can safely conclude that Ah Bam was the respected head of an extended clan. If the codex as we have it was written in the early 1740s and is the original manuscript, we can conclude that Ah Bam was probably born around 1680.

Besides all his duties as an elder, he had to have found time to keep a *milpa* throughout his life, a plot of ground where he grew corn, beans, sweet potatoes, and squash. Rich or poor, aristocrat or commoner, to be a true Maya who keeps to traditional ways, a man needed to have and to work his *milpa*, for the maize plant was a god.

Although ostensibly Christianized, the Mayas secretly retained much of their traditional religion. Ancient rituals continued to be performed in the family circle, in private gatherings, and in the fields of the *milpas*. In this way Ah Bam must have been completely in accord with the old religion and was surely a practitioner. These texts contain transcriptions of old songs and poems that Ah Bam must have heard and sung in those secret gatherings where the old culture was kept alive. He was not alone in writing down the ancient lore. Mayas in every town translated their old hieroglyphic books into alphabetic writing—the *Books of Chilam Balam*—and read them out loud in secret gatherings, where the old songs were sung and chanted accompanied by a drum and where, on special occasions, ancient plays were performed. No ancient Mayan drama from Yucatan has survived, but one has come down to us from the Guatemala highlands, the Rabinal Achí.

Dzitbalche is a small town a few kilometers south of Calkini, the ancient capital of the province formerly known as Canul, stretching for about seventy kilometers along the western coast of the Yucatan peninsula above the city of Campeche. In ancient times Dzitbalche was an important town due to its proximity to the capital and its location on the main road, which followed along the western foot of the Puuc hills.

When the Spaniards arrived, Yucatan was divided into fifteen chiefdoms, each ruled by a hereditary *batab*, a political-military chief, also known as a *halach uinic* ("a true man") or *ahau* (lord). This arrangement had been in place since the fall of Mayapan a hundred years earlier, around the year 1441. Each *batab* lived in his capital city or center. In the surrounding territory were smaller self-governing towns and villages (*cah'oob*), each run by a town chief, a *holpop*, appointed by the *batab*. Among the *holpop*'s duties was to be lead singer and chanter in ceremonies and to be in charge of the musical instruments of the town. The *ah kulel* was the first assistant and advisor to the *holpop* and therefore the second most important and powerful person in the town, at least politically. Musical ability was one of the most important qualifications needed to rise to those positions. The *holpop* and the *ah kulel* were also poets and composers of songs.

Lineage (*chibal*) as well as ability determined social position among the Yucatec Mayas, both before and after the Conquest. Each province of Yucatan was organized around its "first" and "second" lineages, which together traditionally held the most important public positions. Dzitbalche is located in the old province of Canul, in which the Canuls were the first lineage. A Canul was always the *batab* (provincial chief) and he ordinarily appointed a Canche as his *ah kulel* (assistant, second in power). This arrangement was usually reflected on the local level. The *batab* usually appointed a Canul as *holpop* (village chief) and a Canche as village *ah kulel*. The Canul lineage were descendants of Mexicans originally invited into Mayapan from Tabasco as a garrison. The Canches were the second lineage of the province, below only the Canuls. However, in some circumstances the *batab* might appoint a member of the second lineage as *holpop* instead of a first lineage candidate.

When Mayapan, the centralized capital of Yucatan, was abandoned in 1441, all the lineages dispersed and founded independent provinces. The Chronicle of Calkini tells us that the leaders of the Canul and Canche lineages, Tzab Canul and Namay Canche, led their people to jointly found the province of Canul, with the capital at Calkini, not far

*A chief (*batab *or* halach-uinic*) dressed in ceremonial attire of the era of Ah Bam.*
Books of Chilam Balam of Chumayal.

from Mayapan to the north and Dzitbalche to the south. Tzab Canul was the first *batab* at Calkini, and Namay Canche was his *ah kulel*. Several years later Tzab Canul appointed Namay Canche to be *holpop* of Dzitbalche, despite the fact that the latter was of the secondary lineage. After that, Canches succeeded each other as *holpop* of Dzitbalche generation after generation. At the time of the writing of the Chronicle of Calkini (1579), the narrator, Alonso Canche, tells us that his father, Napot Canche, was then the current *holpop* of Dzitbalche.

Let us return to the byline of the Songs of Dzitbalche: "This book was written by the honorable Mr. Bam, great-grandson of the great *ah kulel* of the town of Dzitbalche in the year 1440."

The first phrase in Mayan is *"Laiil h'an altteah dzib taan tun men yum h' Ah Bam."*

Altteah is equivalent to *analte*, which means a traditional Mayan screenfold "book" made of bark surfaced with white lime and written in hieroglyphics. The Mayan word for a Spanish book is *"hu'n."* So Ah Bam does not does not actually call this a book, but a traditional screenfold.

THE LIFE OF AH BAM

"*Men yum h' Ah Bam.*" *Men* is a verb root which means "to do or make something" and also refers to a native priest or shaman; today in Yucatan a shaman is still called a *hmen* or "one who does." *Yum* means "father" or "the honorable." *Ah* is the equivalent of "mister." *Bam* is a shortened form of *Balam,* meaning "jaguar," like the great Chilam (priest) Balam, famous for his prophesies, whose name graces the *Books of Chilam Balam.* Together with the internal evidence of the attitudes expressed in the poems, his very name strongly indicates that Ah Bam was probably a *chilam*, a native priest.

Ah Bam does not give his family or lineage (*chibal*) name, but he had to have been either a Canul or a Canche. The great-grandfather mentioned easily might have been Namay Canche, the famed *ah kulel* who led the Canche lineage out of Mayapan when that great city fell and who later became *holpop* of Dzitbalche. The term "great-grandfather" does not necessarily refer strictly to only four generations, but could simply mean "ancestor."

The very fact that Ah Bam signs his name to his *analte* book may seem unusual for an Amerindian of his time, since artists are traditionally anonymous in many Amerindian cultures. But writers were not always anonymous in ancient Mayan society. The concept of authorship was part of the culture. A Mayan scribe-writer-artist, known as *ah dzib*, signed his work with the glyph "*u dzib,*" "his writing," followed by the author's name. Sculptors had an equivalent way of signing their works. The *ah dzib* was scribe, writer, and artist at the same time. There were no distinctions. The *ah dzib'oob* belonged to the nobility, and their work brought them high status.

Ah Bam does not give the year in the Spanish form, but as "*hum pic hum baak ca kaatun,*" that is, "one *pic*, one *baak*, two *katun'oob.*" The date is in the Mayan counting system. The Mayas were constantly refining their calendar count, so there are several possibilities for the equivalent date in our calendar. Mayan counting was primarily by twenties instead of by tens; however there were variations in the calendar count. A *pic* is equal to 20 x 20 x 20, or 8,000, but in the colonial era it was usually

Author's signature in ancient Mayan script: u dzib, "his writing."

considered the equivalent of a millennium, or 1,000 years. A *bac* is equal to 20 x 20, or 400 years. A *katun* is equal to 7,200 days (20 x 20 x 18), almost 20 years, so two *katun'oob* equal about 40 years. If a *pic* is considered 1,000 instead of 8,000, the year is 1440 A.D.

That date can be read two ways: to refer to the time when Ah Bam wrote the book or when his great grandfather was *ah kulel*. Since 1440 was before the arrival of the Spaniards, it cannot possibly be the year the book was written, at least in alphabetic form. It is possible that it was written in hieroglyphic Mayan in that year and later translated into alphabetic Mayan, but that is highly speculative. It is also possible that 1440 is a mistake, but since the Mayas were so very concerned with accuracy in dating, that is doubtful. A more probable interpretation is that 1440 refers to the time when Ah Bam's great-grandfather—or other ancestor—was *ah kulel*, first advisor to the chief.

Why single out that one year? Because that was the last year before the fall of the great city of Mayapan, a watershed event in Mayan history. The most important lineages in Yucatan all proudly traced their descent and authority back to Mayapan, the only centralized and unified Mayan government Yucatan had ever seen, founded by the legendary leader Kukulcan (Feathered Serpent). Out of a time of chaos, constant war, insecurity, and poverty, the rule of Kukulcan and the Itzas had brought order, peace, security, and prosperity. Culture and the arts once more flourished. Forever after, the heyday of Mayapan was remembered with reverence by the Mayas of Yucatan as a golden age and Kukulcan as the epitome of a wise, benevolent, almost godlike ruler.

So by saying that his great-grandfather was *ah kulel* during the era of Mayapan, Ah Bam is endowing him with the highest authority, respect, and credibility, and, as his great-grandson, Ah Bam was receiving this also.

However, many Mayas did not look favorably on some of Kukulcan's successors and came to view the later Itzas with resentment, as foreign interlopers.

When the Spaniards conquered Yucatan, they did not abolish the native aristocracy at first but, on the contrary, confirmed the power structure of the old system for those Mayan nobles who were willing to cooperate in the new power system. The Spaniards simply reappointed the cooperative *batab'oob*, *holpop'oob*, and *ah kulel'oob* to the positions they already held, and replaced any who resisted.

When the conqueror Montejo arrived in the province of Canul in 1541, the *batab* Nachan Canul went into hiding, leaving his *ah kulel*, Napot Canche, to officially meet the Spaniards. Because of this, Montejo appointed Napot Canche as governor instead of Nachan Canul. After that a Canche was always governor of the province in the Spanish colonial system, but to the Mayas a Canul remained the real *batab* of Canul province.

Whether Ah Bam was a Canche or a Canul, and many other questions about his life, may be cleared up by further research. Somewhere in the annals of Dzitbalche or Calkini there is probably much more information about Ah Bam, waiting for someone to dig it out.

The Sacred Hymns of Pachacuti

ANCIENT INCA POETRY

Portrait of Pachacuti. Rostworowski de Díaz Canseco, Pachacutec Inca Yupanqui.

INTRODUCTION

THE SACRED HYMNS OF PACHACUTI

THE LIFE OF PACHACUTI INCA YUPANQUI

INTRODUCTION

The hymns of Pachacuti Inca Yupanqui, composed for the Situa ceremony around 1440-1450, are among the world's great sacred poetry.

The eleven hymns, or *haillikuna*, in Quechua verse were sung to the accompaniment of instruments during the annual Inca ceremony of the Situa Raymi, held at the first new moon after the spring equinox.

Pachacuti, the great Inca emperor, transformed the vision of the first Inca, Manco Capac, into Tawantinsuyu, Land of the Four Directions, the Inca empire.

In appreciation of the sacred Inca hymns, the great Quechua scholar Jesús Lara wrote, "Among the hymns . . . there are fragments of profound beauty, interpreters of a high level of spirituality reached by the Inca people. Many of them seduce by their transparent simplicity, for the elemental gratitude in them for the deity who creates and governs, who grants sustenance, peace, and happiness. Many captivate through their otherworldly, metaphysical status. All by the emotional force that resides in them" (*Poesia quechua* 74; my translation).

INCA POETS, POETRY, AND MUSIC

Traditions of poetry and song were deeply ingrained in Inca culture, encompassing both sacred and secular forms shared by the common people and the aristocracy. Prayer songs, ceremonial songs, work songs, and love songs were part of the texture of daily life. Poetry, music, and dance were integral to all the great Inca religious festivals. Each region throughout the empire retained its language and culture and cultivated its own fine arts, as well as taking on the superimposed Quechua and Inca culture. On special occasions theatrical dramas were performed with interludes of poetry and music. Only one complete ancient Inca drama has come down to us, the great *Apu Ollantay*, in which Pachacuti is a major character.

Sacred *haillikuna*, or hymns, were prayers and philosophical ponderings. Inca priests greeted each sunrise and sunset singing *haillikuna*, usually accompanied by music, beseeching Tiqsi Wiracocha (the Creator), Inti (the sun), Illapa (thunder-lightning), Pachamama (the Earth Mother), Mamaquilla (the moon), and all the *wakakuna* (spirits of places) to grant health, prosperity, and happiness to the people, the Inca, and the empire. Sacred hymns were usually composed by poets who were also priests.

While the Incas are usually thought of as sun worshipers, in reality their worship focused more on Wiracocha, the Creator. The sun was the tangible manifestation, but the invisible Wiracocha was above the sun, just as his golden icon was placed higher than the Sun's on the many-tiered stage they erected in the center of the great plaza at Cuzco during festivals. The primary invocation in all but two of these hymns is addressed to Wiracocha. Many of these same hymns are secondarily consecrated to the other deities. Besides Wiracocha, only Pachamama (Earth Mother, in hymn 9) and Inti (the Sun, in hymn 10) are invoked alone. The most important *wakakuna* were physical manifestations of Wiracocha at various shrines. Wiracocha was the immanent and omnipresent creator and maintainer of the world and of the other deities. His numerous attributes and aspects included Pachawallpaq, world creator; Pachakama, world governor; and Pachayachachiq, world teacher. He was a gentle, benevolent deity, forever bearing gifts for humankind, keeping the people safe and at peace.

The Inca founder Manco Capac, like Pachacuti, was a poet. Three of Manco's *haillikuna* survive. We have sacred hymns from a few other Inca emperors too, Capac Yupanqui (the fifth Sapa Inca), Inca Ruca (the sixth) and Huascar (the twelfth). The *haillikuna* of Manco and Inca Ruca are prayers, while those of Capac Yupanqui and Huascar are exorcisms of offending *wakakuna*. In addition we know that both Manco and Pachacuti not only composed *haillikuna* but also invented in other verse forms.

The sacred *hailli* was considered the highest poetic form. There were secular *haillikuna* as well. *Haillikuna* encompassed historical and agricultural modes and themes. Heroic hymns celebrated the military exploits of the Inca kings and warriors. Unfortunately, no heroic *haillikuna* have survived, but we have a number of anonymous agricultural hymns. These *haillikuna* were sung by the working people during sowing and harvesting, particularly during collective work in the fields of the sun and of the Inca, the fields that formed the common stores that were distributed to the people in years of poor harvests and supported the religious establishment and the governing aristocracy.

There were many other forms of poetry and song. *Taki*, the generic term for "song," encompassed a variety of styles and subjects. The *arawi* was a love song, the *wawaki* a dialog in verse. The *wayñu, qhashwa, samak'uika,* and *qharuyu* were songs for different dances. Two poetry forms were often recited without music: *wankakuna* (elegies or laments) and *aranwaykuna* (humorous verses usually performed as part of a larger theater piece). Composers were both aristocrats and commoners.

Inca poets *(arawikuqkuna)* composed in the usual full spectrum of poets' concerns. Usually accompanied by music, they sung of love, life, spirituality, politics, of the gods and heroes, the dignity and trials of work, of working the soil. A good number of their works have come down to us in a variety of forms. Unfortunately, most are anonymous. The Emperor-poets are the only ones whose authorship and biographies have been preserved.

Quechua poets liked their verses brief and without obvious artifice. *Arawikuqkuna* did not care about metrics and scorned technical rigidity. The meters of their verses were determined by the inner necessities of meaning and poetics. Inside the forms of the songs there was great flexibility. The rhythm was the natural fluidity of the language. The number of syllables in each line was highly mutable. A line of poetry usually consisted of only five or six syllables, and rarely more than eight. Rhyme and assonance were common but not necessary. Many Quechua words have the same endings. Blank verses were common.

An Inca musical group included drums, ocarinas, tambourines, bells, trumpets (of conch, gourd, ceramic, or wood), and bean shell anklets (worn by dancers). In Cuzco, *haillikuna* were sometimes accompanied by a group of women playing golden drums set with precious stones. Andean music today, noted throughout the world, is rooted in the music of Inca times. Now as then, the flute, played on a pentatonic scale in a minor key, provides its most distinctive sound.

Pachacuti's Other Works

Besides the eleven *haillikuna* of the Situa, his only surviving works are his aphorisms and laws and his deathbed poem, as well as the title of a song for the Capac Raymi.

Aphorisms and Laws

Transmitted by Garcilaso El Inca in Spanish translation, we have a series of Pachacuti's aphorisms and laws, among which are:

"He who envies the good draws evil from them for himself, just as the spider draws poison from flowers."

"Drunkenness, rage, and madness are similar, but the first two are voluntary and transformable, the third permanent."

"The noble and courageous man is known by his patience in adversity. Impatience is a sign of a vulgar and low mind, badly taught and worse trained."

"Governors should mind two things with great attention: first, they and their subjects should observe and fulfill the emperor's laws perfectly; second, they should consider with great vigilance and care the common and particular resources of their province."

"One who cannot govern his house and family will be much less competent to govern a state, and should not be given power over others."

"The physician or herbalist who is ignorant of the virtues of herbs, or who knows the virtues of some but does not seek to know the virtues of all, knows little or nothing. He must work until he knows them all, whether useful or injurious, in order to deserve the title he claims."

"He who seeks to count the stars before he can count the sums and knots of the quipus deserves derision" (my translation).

Song for the Capac Raymi

Pachacuti not only composed *haillikuna* but also cast his poetic inventions in other verse forms.

During the ceremonies of Capac Raymi, "Feast of the First Inca," so-called because it was initiated by Manco Capac, young Inca noblemen passed a series of trials to win their first arms. The initiate dancers would dress in red shirts with red and white fringes down to their feet, and puma skins were draped over those, with the heads and necks covering their own. Accompanied by conch shell trumpets, they sang and performed the *taki* (song) titled "Wari." This song was given to Manco Capac by the Creator, along with a command that it be sung only at this ceremony. Two hundred years later Pachacuti expanded the ceremony, as he did many others, and added the *taki* titled "Coyo," which he composed (or received as poets have always received their poems). "Coyo" was performed with drums twice a day for six days during the initiation. No written trace remains of the lyrics of either "Wari" or "Coyo," but for all we know, they might still be sung somewhere in the Andes today.

THE DEATHBED POEM

Pachacuti composed and sang his last poem, his final words, on his deathbed. A Spanish translation of it is included in *Historia de los Incas,* written in 1572 by Pedro Sarmiento de Gamboa, one of the most sympathetic and accurate of the conquistador chroniclers. I have included it in his biography.

THE QUECHUA (RUNASIMI) LANGUAGE

Quechua—or, more properly, Runasimi, meaning literally "People Mouth"—is an agglutinative language, adding syllables onto a root to form long, meaningful words. By the addition of small particles to Quechua verbs, one can express numerous subtleties of thought and emotion. Many words have several synonyms, each with a slight twist of meaning. Runasimi contains many onomatopoetic words. Although outlawed for a period by the Spaniards after the revolt of Tupac Amaru II, Quechua survived and has about seven million speakers today. It is described by native speakers as an extraordinarily expressive idiom.

Quechua was not the original language of the Incas. The Inca aristocracy actually spoke a private language among themselves, most likely a related language of the same family. Quechua was probably first spoken in ancient times in small chiefdoms in the Abancay River valley, east of Cuzco. When the Incas emigrated into the Quechua-speaking area of the Cuzco valley around the year 1200, they continued to speak their original language among themselves, but kept it secret and uncomprehended by the common people. The Incas made Quechua into the lingua franca of the empire. Their secret language is now lost, though traces surely remain, perhaps even in these *haillikuna*. Hymn 11 contains the mysterious phrase "Tayna allasto allonto," which no linguist has ever been able to decipher. I have left it in the original. This may be a Quechua phrase garbled by the transcriber, or perhaps it is a special prayer in the private Inca language.

Although the Incas had no actual writing, they carefully recorded and preserved their culture and history, relying on a highly developed mnemonic device, the quipu *(khipu).* The knotted strings of quipus contained chronicles of the past, genealogies, ceremonies, and poetry, as well as accounting and statistical information. Upon the death of an emperor, his successor always had the life and exploits of his predecessor composed into historical ballads and recorded on quipus (the events chosen were, of course, subject to the vagaries of politics). *Khipukamayuqkuna*—professional quipu readers—could access vast quipu libraries which held many keys to the past.

Though most of the quipus were quickly destroyed by the Spaniards, a number of them survived the flames and exist today. However, the ability to really read their complexities died with the last Inca *khipukamayuq*. Even if the tradition had not been so violently terminated, basic questions of interpretation would remain, human memory

A reader with a quipu. Poma de Ayala, Nueva crónica y buen gobierno.

being more variable than the written word. A simplified form of quipu, the "tally cord," is used by Quechua llama shepherds today. In the Huarochirí community, and probably in others, each clan *(ayllu)* owns ancient quipus, which are used as sacred ritual objects in the investiture of power to community offices in their traditional political system.

NAMES AND ATTRIBUTES OF WIRACOCHA IN THE *HAILLIKUNA*

Pachacuti tried to bond all the diverse tribes and nations that had become provinces of Tawantinsuyu into a new unified nation. Toward this end he promoted the worship of the Creator, Wiracocha (Wiraqocha), over all other deities and *wakakuna* (spirits of places). Instead of trying to replace regional and local deities, Pachacuti had them assimilated into Wiracocha. The Creator adopted the names, attributes, and *wakakuna* of the principal deities of the provinces. In most cases this was no problem, since many of these deities already were creator gods and gift-bringers. They assimilated into Wiracocha without losing their original names and attributes. Pachacuti used the Situa and the other annual Inca ceremonies and poem-prayer-songs in this cultural revolution.

Below are some of the other names and attributes of Wiracocha, many of which can be found in various *haillikuna*:

Kamaq, churaq = molder, maker; he who infuses life and sets all things in order

Tiqsi (Teqse) = cause, origin, root, foundation, beginning of all

Qaylla = end of all

Pachaq ch'ulla = unique in this world

Ukhu ch'ulla = unique in the underworld

Tawapaka = fortunate

Kusi usapuq hayllipu = lucky, happy, victorious

Illa = shining, flashing, gleaming

Tukapu aknupu = elegantly, showily dressed

Wallpay wana; Wallparillaq = industrious, diligent worker

T'itu = provider

Qhon = thunder crash (onomatopoetic)

Wiraqochaya = my Wiracocha

Apu = earth spirit, sacred mountain; "Lord"

Apuqochan = lord of the lake = *Apotinuiracochan* = *waka* (spirit of place) at Ayabamba, beyond Tambo

Atun (Hatun, Hatun apu) Wiracocha = lord without measure = *waka* at Urcos

Chanka (Chuquichanka) Wiracocha = lord of mountains = *waka* at Hyaypar

Corcos Wiracocha = *waka* at Ayabamba

Urusayua Wiracocha = *waka* at Ayabamba

Aksa Wiracocha = lord of prayers = *waka* (location unknown)

Kuniraya Wiracocha = originally Kuniraya, deity of the Warachiri

Tunapa Wiracocha = originally Tunapa, deity of the Titicaca region

Pachawallpaq Wiracocha = world creator

Pachakama Wiracocha = world governor

Pachayachachiq Wiracocha = world teacher

The root meanings of the name "Wiracocha" have been debated by many scholars. "Qocha" in Quechua means "ocean" or "lake;" "Wira" means "fat" or "grease" (by extension: abundant, healthy, successful). "Wiraqocha" is used in Quechua today when speaking very formally, to mean "Lord," "Sir," or "Mister."

SIMPLIFIED GUIDE TO QUECHUA PRONUNCIATION

Vowels and consonants in general as in Spanish.
>sh and w as in English
>q as ch in Scottish *loch*

Glottalized and plosive consonants:
>ch', k', p', q' and t' are pronounced by holding the breath (closing the glottis), then releasing it and pronouncing the letter with a sudden unsticking of the tongue or lips

Aspirated consonants:
>chh, kh, ph, qh, th are pronounced with a small puff of air after the letter.

Older spellings include:
>tt = t'
>c = k, k', kh
>cc = q, q', qh

Accent is usually on the penultimate syllable.

Quechua sentences are built around root words, to which the rest of the meaning is added by attaching affixes. Usual sentence word order is subject-object-verb, but word order is flexible, and any word can go first depending on what is being emphasized. Questions are indicated by the insertion of a syllable, not with rising intonation as in English.

Linguistic Guide to Quechua Pronunciation

	phoneme	alphabetic representation	
vowels	/ä/	ah	
	/e/	i	(before or after consonants q, q', or qh)
	/ü/	u, uw	
	/ȯ/	u	(before or after consonants q, q', or qh)

	phoneme	Quechua	
consonants	/ch/	ch	
	/f/	ph	
	/g/	g	
	/h/	h	
	/k/	k, q	
	/k/	k, q, p	(at end of word, like Scottish loch)
	/l/	l	
	/lʸ/	ll	(with middle of tongue against roof of mouth)
	/m/	m	
	/n/	n	
	/nʸ/	ñ	(as in Spanish)
	/p/	p	
	/ɾ/	r	(flap sound as in American English better; like a very short –d sound)
	/r/	rr	(as in Spanish, trilled r)
	/s/	s	
	/sh/	sh	
	/t/	t	
	/w/	w	
	/y/	y	

Diphthongs: The Quechua writing system combines the letters *w* and *y* with *a*, *i*, or *u* to form the following diphthongs.

	phoneme	Quechua	
dipthongs	/aw/	aw	
	/ai/	ay	
	/yü/	iw	
	/ā/	ay	(before or after q, q', or qh)
	/üi/	uy	
	/oi/	uy	(before or after q, q', or qh)

THE SACRED HYMNS OF THE SITUA

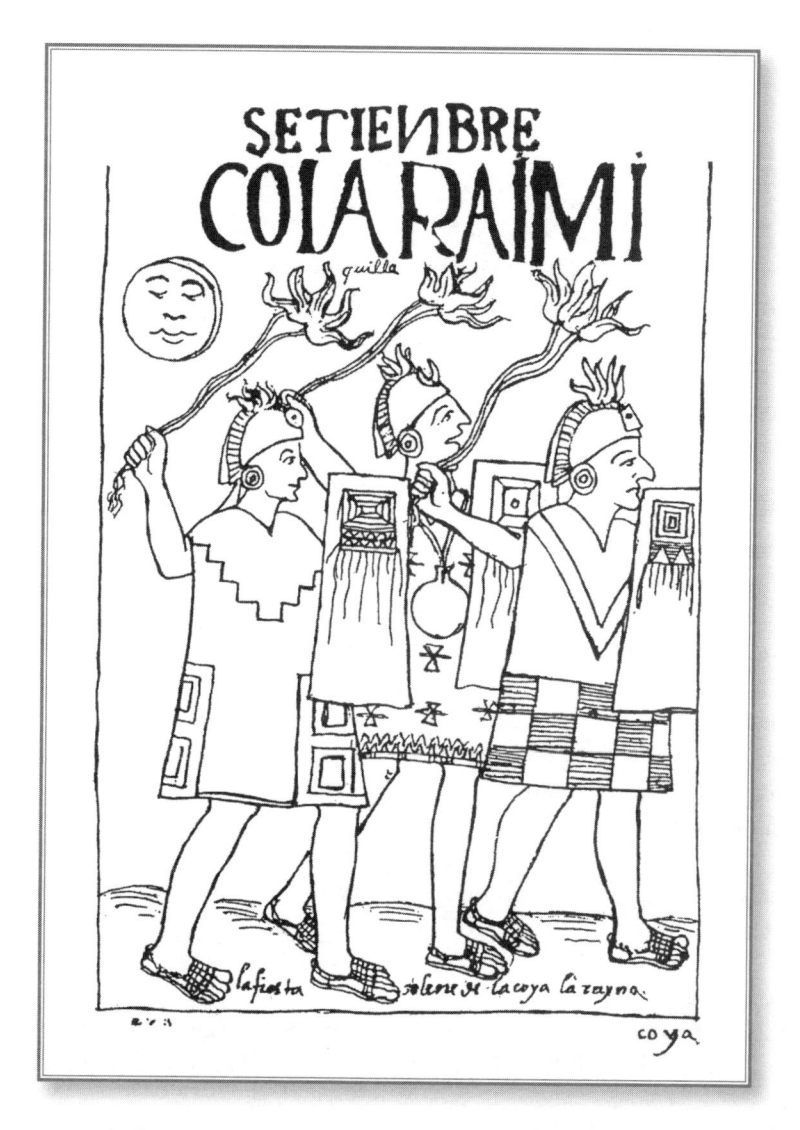

The Situa ceremony. The accompanying text reads, "The men presented themselves fully armed and formed up in companies, as if they were going into battle. They fired their slingshots into the air or simply flung burning torches. At the same time they shouted to the diseases at the tops of their voices, telling them to go away and leave the villages in peace and quiet." Poma de Ayala, Nueva crónica y buen gobierno.

The Incas kept both a solar and a lunar calendar and used a combination of the two to determine their main annual festivals, which were related to the agricultural cycle. The Situa Raymi, Brilliant Feast, was a purification ceremony held at the first new moon after the spring equinox.

Situa Raymi came in the lunar month of Coya-Raymi, the Queen's Feast. The Queen was Mamaquilla, Mother Moon, the Sun's bride and Queen of all the stars and planets. This was her month and began with her feast. The highest Inca women and the Virgins of the Moon played central roles in the ceremonies. Coya-Raymi was a month for sowing and planting. It was also a time when the previous year's stores were running low. In years of thin harvests Coya-Raymi was the season when hunger began to set in.

The rainy season also began at this moment, and the first rains often brought sickness to the people. Pachacuti Inca Yupanqui instituted the Situa to ask the Creator Wiracocha and the other deities to protect them from sickness. The Situa honored and invoked the Creator, Sun, Thunder, the *wakakuna*, and—on one particular day—the Moon and Earth Mother Pachamama.

To determine the equinox they used tall carved stone columns that Pachacuti had erected in the middle of a large stone ring in the great central square in Cuzco, in front of the Temple of the Sun. Across the middle of the ring a line was drawn east to west. Every day the Sun Priests took careful daily observations of the columns' shadows. When the shadows fell exactly along the line and at midday cast almost no shadow, they decked the columns with flowers and aromatic herbs, placed the golden throne of the Sun on top of the column and showered it with offerings of gold, silver, and precious stones.

The Virgins of the Sun made enormous quantities of *sanku*, little round loaves of half-baked, roughly ground corn dough the size of a peach, cooked briefly in dry pots. They made *sanku* only twice a year, for the sacrifices of Situa and for the Sun Feast, Inti-Raymi, the greatest of Inca festivals, which took place at the winter solstice, three months earlier. As the seasons are reversed in the southern hemisphere, Inti-Raymi was in June and Situa in September.

On the day of the new moon that began the month of Coya-Raymi, at high noon, the Inca and all the chiefs of his council and the other principal lords went to the Curicancha, the House of Gold, the Temple of the Sun, the very heart of Cuzco and the Inca world. There they determined how the Situa would be celebrated that year. At that very time chiefs and priests all over the Inca empire were doing the same to prepare for their local ceremonies and sending delegations to the capital with llamas and the icons of their *wakakuna*.

On the first day of the moon after the equinox all able-bodied citizens began a three-day fast with only a little raw corn and water, and abstained from sex. During this time they baked the special loaves of *sanku*, into which they mixed a few drops of blood obtained by pricking the skin of a child between five and ten years old between the eyebrows. All infirm people and foreigners had to leave the city. To assure quiet, dogs were taken out beyond city limits.

To begin the ceremony, a group of four hundred armed men assembled in the square in front of the Sun Temple. The icons of the Creator and Thunder were brought from their own temples to the Temple of the Sun to join the icon of the Sun. The Sun Priest came out of the Temple and proclaimed the feast to the assembly.

From the Fort of the Sun on Sacsayhuaman, the high fortress behind Cuzco, a richly dressed Inca, wrapped in a blanket and holding a spear with a band of colored feathers attached at different points with rings of gold, ran down to the main square and met four other Incas similarly dressed. He touched his spear to theirs and said that the Sun had told them to go forth as his messengers to expel the diseases.

The four hundred armed men walked to the great golden urn near the center of the square, crying, "O sickness, disasters, misfortunes, and dangers, leave this land!" One hundred faced in each of the four directions and cried, "Away all evils, all evils away!"

Each group left the square running to one of the four directions. As they passed, every person in Cuzco came to the door, shaking her or his mantle or cloak, crying, "Let the evils be gone. We have greatly desired this festival. Wiracocha, Creator of all, let us live another year, so we can see another feast like this!"

Each of the groups of armed men followed their four roads to nearby villages, where they passed the cry onto others waiting there. These in turn ran to the next village and ultimately to a river where they bathed and washed their clothes and weapons. The four rivers would carry the evils away and empty them into the sea.

When all had returned to Cuzco, music and dancing began. All danced, including the emperor, then went to bathe in rivers and fountains. That night they lit large straw torches and passed them one to another in the streets, and shot rocks from slings into the air.

Finally back at their houses, each rubbed some *sanku* corn dough on his or her face, then over their doorways and in places where they stored food and clothes. They threw some into the fountains, saying, "Keep us free from sickness. May no sickness enter this house." Each sent some *sanku* to their relations and friends. The Incas put *sanku* on the mummies of the ancestors of their lineages, whom they preserved and worshipped.

The next day everyone feasted and drank *chicha*, beer made of boiled white corn; everyone shared in the feast, even the poorest, and no one was permitted to quarrel.

That night the priests washed the icons (*wakakuna*) of the Sun, the Creator, the Thunder, and the Inca tribal *waka* Huanacauri and rubbed *sancu* on them to warm them. Likewise, each clan lineage washed the mummies of their ancestors and rubbed them with *sancu*. In the morning the priests and lineage elders placed their best foods before the *wakakuna* and mummies, then ate the foods.

That morning the Inca, his wife, and the lords all came into the great plaza dressed in finery. The Sun priests brought out the principal icon of the Sun, called Apupunchau, Lord of Day, with two gold figures of the Sun. Several women came forward: those with the titles Inca-Ocllo and Palla-Ocllo, followed by the Coya-Facsa, the daughter or wife of the Inca dedicated to the Sun. They placed the image of the Sun on his golden bench in the plaza. The priests of the Creator, the Thunder, and the principal *waka* Huanacauri brought out their icons and the richly dressed mummies of their ancestors and placed them on their golden seats.

The entire population then came out, dressed in their best clothes, and passed the day in eating, drinking, and other enjoyments. Dressed in red shirts down to their feet, with garlands of flowers on their heads, accompanied by musical canes, which made a music called *tika-tika*, they danced the *taki* (song) called "Alansitua Saki." They gave thanks first to the Creator, then to the Sun and the Thunder, for having spared them, and prayed for another healthy year.

The Sapa Inca, with the Sun image before him, came forth with a great gold goblet of *chicha*, which he handed to the priest, who in turn emptied it into the golden urn. The *chicha* passed through the urn to a pipe below, which took it to the houses of the Sun, the Thunder, and the Creator.

The next day they assembled again as before, but bringing a huge flock of llamas, which had been transported to Cuzco from all corners of the empire. These were the flocks of the Creator, the Thunder, and the Sun, raised on lands set aside for them. All were without any blemish and had never been shorn. The sun priest selected four of the most perfect and sacrificed them to the Creator, the Sun, the Thunder, and the *waka* Huanacauri.

The priest had *sanku* spread on large golden plates and sprinkled it with llama blood, making *yahuar-sanku*. The priest said, "Take care how you eat this *sanku*; whoever eats it in sin and with a double will and heart is seen by our father the Sun, who will punish him with grievous troubles. Whoever eats it with a single heart, the Sun will favor him and reward him, will grant children and happy years and all that he requires."

All stood and vowed never to speak against the Creator, the Sun, or the Thunder, and never to be false to their Lord Inca, on penalty of condemnation and trouble.

The priest of the Sun took some *sanku* in three fingers and ate it. One by one everyone followed, even the littlest children.

The priests then killed the four sacrificial llamas and looked for signs on their inflated lungs. From these signs they judged whether or not the year would be prosperous. They burned the sacrificial llamas before the Creator, the Sun, and the Thunder, and gave a very small piece of their meat to each person.

The entire flock was then killed and a share of the meat given to every person in Cuzco. As each man entered the square, he pulled off a piece of llama wool and offered it to the Sun.

As the priests distributed the llama meat, they sang the eleven *hailli* prayers, the Sacred Hymns.

The prayers were followed by a great four-day feast of llama meat with vast amounts of *chicha*, continuous music, and *takikuna* (songs). The second day was particularly dedicated to the Creator, the Sun, and Thunder; the fourth day was for the Moon and Earth Mother.

On the fifth day the chiefs and people of all the subject nations came forward with their *wakakuna* and made offerings to the Creator, the Sun, the Thunder, Huanacauri, and the Sapa Inca. The Sun priest sprinkled blood-*sanku* and the chiefs stood and sang the final hymn, a repetition of Hailli 1.

A ticsi Uiracochan	O Creator, root of all,
caylla Uiracochan	Wiracocha, end of all,
tocapo, acnupo Uiracochan,	Lord in shining garments
camac, churac	who infuses life
"Cari cachon	and sets all things in order,
huarmi cachon!"	saying,
nispa.	"Let there be man!
Llutac, rurac,	Let there be woman!"
camascayque,	Molder, maker,
churascaiqui	to all things you have given life:
casilla quespilla cauçamusac.	watch over them,
Maipim canqui?	keep them living prosperously,
Ahuapichu,	fortunately,
ucupichu,	in safety and peace.
puyupichu,	Where are you?
llantupichu?	Outside? Inside?
Hoyarihmay,	Above this world in the clouds?
Hayniguai,	Below this world in the shades?
Ynihuai!	Hear me! Answer me!
Imay pachacama haycay	Take my words to your heart!
pachacama	For ages without end
cauçachihuay,	let me live,
marcarihuay,	grasp me in your arms,
hatallihuay;	hold me in your hands,
cay cullcaitari chasquihuai,	receive this offering
maypis capapis	wherever you are, my Lord,
Viracochaya.	my Wiracocha.

The Sun Priest distributed *sanku* again, and the people ate more llamas. Each nation passed the day singing and dancing their traditional regional *takikuna*. This continued for two days, until the Priest of the Sun distributed the last *sanku,* and the people ate the last llamas. The ceremony of the Situa was then complete.

The Sacred Hymns of Pachacuti

The Inca at the Capac Inti Raymi ceremony, Poma de Ayala, Nueva crónica y buen gobierno.

(1)

Hailli Hoq

A ticsi Uiracochan
caylla Uiracochan
tocapo, acnupo Uiracochan,
camac, churac
"Cari cachon
huarmi cachon!"
nispa.
Llutac, rurac,
camascayque,
churascaiqui
casilla quespilla cauçamusac.
Maipim canqui?
Ahuapichu,
ucupichu,
puyupichu,
llantupichu?
Hoyarihmay,
Hayniguai,
Ynihuai!
Imay pachacama haycay pachacama
cauçachihuay,
marcarihuay,
hatallihuay;
cay cullcaitari chasquihuai,
maypis capapis
Uiracochaya.

(1)

Hymn One

O Creator, root of all,
Wiracocha, end of all,
Lord in shining garments
who infuses life
and sets all things in order,
saying,
"Let there be man!
Let there be woman!"
Molder, maker,
to all things you have given life:
watch over them,
keep them living prosperously,
fortunately
in safety and peace.
Where are you?
Outside? Inside?
Above this world in the clouds?
Below this world in the shades?
Hear me! Answer me!
Take my words to your heart!
For ages without end
let me live,
grasp me in your arms,
hold me in your hands,
receive this offering
wherever you are, my Lord,
my Wiracocha.

(2)

Hailli Iskay
Oración para que multipliquen las jentes

Uiracochan
apacochan
titu Uiracochan
hualpai huana Uiracochan
toparo acnupo Uiracochan:
runa yachachuchun,
huarma yachachuchun,
mirachun llactapacha,
casilla quispilla cachun.
Camascayquita guacaychay
atalli,
ymay pachacama haycay,
pachacama.

(2)

Hymn Two
Prayer That the People May Multiply

> Creator
> Lord of the Lake,
> Wiracocha provider,
> industrious Wiracocha
> in shining clothes:
> Let man live well,
> let woman live well,
> let the peoples multiply,
> live blessed and prosperous lives.
> Preserve what you have infused
> with life
> for ages without end,
> hold it in your hand.

(3)

HAILLI KINSA
A TODAS LAS HUACAS

Caylla Uiracochan
ticçi Uiracochan
hapacochan
hualpai huana Uiracochan
chanca Uiracochan
acxa Uiracochan
atun Uiracochan
caylla Uiracochanta
cancuna aynichic hunichic:
Llaota runa yachacuc ccapac
hahuaypi hucupi purispapas.

(3)

Hymn Three
To all the wakakuna

Creator, end of all things
root of all
Lord of the Lake
active diligent Wiracocha,
Lord of Mountains
Lord of Prayers
Lord of Rituals
Lord without measure,
Creator, end of all,
who rewards and grants:
Let the communities
and peoples prosper
and also those who journey
outside or within.

(4)

HAILLI TAWA

O Uiracochan
cusi ussapo chayllipo Uiracochaya
runa caya may da
caymi runa yana huacchaquisa
runayqui camascayqui
churascayqui:
casi quispilla camuchun
huarmayhuan churinhuan
chin canta;
ama guatquintaguan yayaichichu
unay huasa causachun
mana allcas, mamana pitispa
micumuchun, upiamuchun.

(4)

Hymn Four

O Lord
fortunate, happy,
victorious Wiracocha,
merciful and compassionate
toward the people:
Before you stand
your servants and the poor
to whom you have given life
and put in their places:
Let them be happy and blessed
with their children
and descendants;
let them not fall into veiled dangers
along the lonely road;
let them live many years
without weakening or loss,
let them eat, let them drink.

Hailli Pisqa

O Uiraccochaya
ticçi Uiracochaya,
hualparillac
camac, churac
"Cay hurin pachape micuchun
upiachun," nispa.
Churascayquicta
camascayquicta
micuinin yachachun papa cara
ymaymana miconcan cachon,
niscayqueta camachic micachic
mana muchuncanpac
mana muchuspacanta
ynincampo
amacaçachuncho
amachupichichuncho
casilla huacaychamuy.

(5)

Hymn Five

O my Lord,
my Creator, origin of all,
diligent worker
who infuses life and order
into all,
saying, "Let them eat,
let them drink in this world":
Increase the potatoes and corn,
all the foods
of those to whom you have given
life,
whom you have established.
You who order,
who fulfill what you have decreed,
let them increase.
So the people do not suffer and,
not suffering, believe in you.
Let it not frost
let it not hail,
preserve all things in peace.

(6)

Hailli Soqta
Oración al Sol

Uiracochaya
"Punchao cachunto, tacachun,"
nispac nic;
"Pacarichun yllarichun,"
nispac nic;
Punchao churiyquicta casillacta
quispillacta purichic
runa rurascay quicta
canchay canchay uncancampac
Uiracochaya.
Casilla quispilla punchao Iynga
runa yanani o hiscayquicta
quillari canchari
ama honcochispa, ama
nanachispa
caçicta quispicha huacaychaspa.

(6)

Hymn Six
Prayer to the Sun

Lord Wiracocha,
Who says,
"Let there be day,
let there be night!"
Who says,
"Let there be dawn,
let it grow light!"
Who makes the Sun, your son,
move happy and blessed each day,
so that man whom you have made
has light:
My Wiracocha,
shine on your Inca people,
illuminate your servants,
whom you have shepherded,
let them live
happy and blessed
preserve them
in peace,
free of sickness, free of pain.

(7)

HAILLI QANCHIS
ORACIÓN POR YNGA

A Uiracochan
ticçi Uiracochan
gualpay huana Uiracochan
atun Uiracochan
tarapaca Uiracochan
"Capac cachun, Ynca cachun,"
nispac nu:
Capac churaspacquicta
Ynca camascayquicta,
casillacta quispollacta
huacaychamuy.
Runan yanan yachachuchun.
Aoca ripunari usachun
ymaypacha, haycay
pachacama
ama allca chispa
churinta mitantaguanpas
huacaychaychay caçiccaccllacta
Uiracochaya.

(7)

Hymn Seven
Prayer for the Inca

O Lord Wiracocha,
origin of all things,
diligent Lord,
Creator beyond measure,
Fortunate Wiracocha
Who says, "Let there be lords,
let there be Incas:"
Preserve the Lord you have raised,
the Inca you have given life,
preserve him blessed and safe.
Let the people, his servants,
live well.
Bring victory over his enemies
for ages without end.
Do not shorten his days,
or his children's or descendants',
keep them fortunate, in peace,
my Lord.

(8)

HAILLI PUSAQ

Uiracochaya
gualpay huana Uiracochaya
runacta casiquispillacta
Capac Inga churiyqui,
guarmayquipac
camascayqui huacay chamuchun.
hatallimuchun
pacha chacam,
runa, llama, micuy
pay captin yacochun.
Capac Ynca camascayquicta
Uiracochaya
ayni,
huni, marcari, hatalli
ymay pachacama.

Hymn Eight

My Lord
diligent worker, Wiracocha:
Preserve the Lord Inca,
your son, your child
him whom you have given life.
Lead him by the hand
happy and blessed.
In all seasons
let the people, the flocks,
all living things,
let them grow.
My Creator:
answer the Lord Inca,
whom you have infused with life,
hear him,
grasp him in your arms,
hold his hand
forever.

(9)

Hailli Isqon

Pachamama
Cuyrumama
Casillacta
Quispillacta:
Capac Ynca
huahuayquicta
marcari,
hatalli.

(9)

HYMN NINE

Pachamama
Earth Mother
Cloud Mother:
Grasp the Lord Inca, your son,
in your arms,
blessed and safe
hold his hand.

(10)

Hailli Chunka
Oración por todos los Yngas

A Punchao Ynca Inti Yayay,
"Cuzco Tambo
cachon aticoc
llasacoc cachun," nispa:
Churac, camac
muchascayqui.
Cusiquispo cachon
amatista
ama llasasca
cachuncho
aticucpac llasa capac
camascayqui,
churascayqui.

(10)

Hymn Ten
Prayer for all the Incas

O Inca Sun, Light, my Father
who says,
"Let them be masters
of Cuzco and Tambo,"
or who says,
"Let them be plundered!":
Orderer, giver of life,
I adore you.
Let us live happily, in peace,
let us not be defeated,
let us not be despoiled,
but let us be masters.
Grant to those you have infused with life
and raised into their places,
grant them abundance and treasures.

(11)

HAILLI CHUNKA-HOQ-NIYOQ
ORACIÓN A TODAS LAS HUACAS

O Pachachulla Uiracochan
ocuchulla Uiracochan
"Huaca uilcacachun," nispa.
Camac
Atun apa
Huaypi huana
"Tayna allasto allonto,"
Uiracochaya,
"Hurinpacha ananpacha
cachon," nispa nic,
ocupa chapi Puca Omacta
chura chay niguai huhiguay
quispi casica musac,
Uiracochaya
micuynioc
mincacyoc
carayoc
Ilamayoc
ymaynayoc
haycaymayoc.
Amacacharihuay cuchu
ymaymana aycaymana
chiquimanta catuiman
manta nacasca
huatusta amusca manta.

(11)

Hymn Eleven
Prayer to all the Wakakuna

O Wiracocha, unique in this world,
Wiracocha, unique in the underworld,
who says,
"Let there be spirits
and lesser spirits."
Life-giver,
Great diligent Lord,
"Tayna allasto allonto,"
my Wiracocha
who says,
"Let there be an underworld;
let there be an upper world,"
commander of the Sun in the underworld,
tell me what you want,
listen to me.
Let me live fortunate and blessed,
my Wiracocha,
with all living things,
with your help,
with corn, with llamas,
with all that exists.
Do not abandon us to all sorts
of maledictions,
sortileges, and spells.

THE LIFE OF PACHACUTI INCA YUPANQUI

(1418-1471)

Pachacuti. Poma de Ayala, *Nueva crónica y buen gobierno.*

The Incas were the last aristocracy in a long line of civilizations dating back many thousands of years in the South American highlands and western coast. The Inca dynasty was founded by the legendary Manco Capac around the year 1200. There are contradictory stories about Manco's origin. One story has him emerging from a cave about eighteen miles southeast of Cuzco, along with three brothers, four sisters, and ten *ayllukuna* (clans or extended families) of followers. According to another story, the Sun created Manco and his siblings on an island in Lake Titicaca, 200 miles away. In either case, believing that they were blessed with special abilities by the benevolent Sun (manifestation of the Creator), Manco and the others left their place of origin in search of a new home in a fertile valley. Arriving in the Cuzco valley, Manco tested the ground with a golden staff and realized that this was the chosen place, Navel of the World. The ruling Inca family and clan adopted a highly structured system of marriage to continue their blood lines. The Sapa Inca was unchallengeable head of the family, clan, and state. With the growing city of Cuzco as his center, Manco invented the core ideas of the Inca order, which his successors perpetuated and developed.

Manco and his wife-sister Mama Ocllo gradually organized and established authority over the neighboring Quechua and Aymara villages. According to legend, Manco taught the people the sciences and arts of the soil, agriculture, husbandry, irrigation, and industries; Ocllo taught spinning, weaving, sewing, all the domestic arts, and the sciences. Manco's only rule at first was for every member of the village or tribe to share in the common labor and its produce, the fruits of the Sun. He instituted an annual work cycle following the seasons. Because people suffered greatly during the cold and wet months, he set up public storehouses whose contents were distributed as relief to all in times of need or calamity. The Sun mandated that the Incas bring this system to the world, so all could benefit from his benevolence.

As well as a culture hero, Manco was a conqueror: clans who refused to accept his power were driven out of the Cuzco valley. However, he never expanded much beyond that immediate area. The region was scattered with small independent city-states, variously fighting and forming alliances. A battle might determine hegemony, but the defeated city would soon re-arm and the cycle would repeat. On this very tenuous basis, through their superior organizational abilities, both economic and military, the Incas became the dominant power in the immediate region. But at the time of Pachacuti's birth two hundred years later, the Incas were still just a small kingdom, still in this same seemingly endless cycle of insecurity.

It was Pachacuti's unique genius to perfect Manco's ideas, to generalize and expand them into an agrarian socialistic system, and to spread them thousands of miles along the west coast of Tawantinsuyu (as the Incas called it) up to Ecuador and down to Chile and Argentina, to the entire known world.

There are conflicting stories about Pachacuti's early life. This account follows the story passed down by most of the chroniclers.

Pachacuti was born about 1418, the third son of Viracocha Inca (the eighth of the dynasty) and Coya Mama Runtu, the Inca's wife and sister. Like all the Inca emperors, Viracocha also had children by many other women.

As a boy Pachacuti was known as Cusi. He and his father did not get along; Viracocha found him unmanageable. His father grew much closer to an "illegitimate" son named Urcon. When Cusi was a teenager, Viracocha decided to send him away from a prince's life in Cuzco to work as a herd boy to the llama and alpaca flocks belonging to the Sun, which were used for wool and in ceremonies. For three years Cusi tended the flocks. Meanwhile, the elderly Viracocha Inca named Urcon as his successor. Succession was through the male line but went to the son who proved himself the most worthy. Selection of a new Sapa Inca had to be approved by the Council of Elders.

One day while Cusi was herding, a stranger came up to him and identified himself as an ancestor, a brother of the first Inca, Manco Capac. The spirit warned Cusi there would be an attack by an enemy. Cusi ran to Cuzco and told his father, but Viracocha Inca refused to listen and just banished him back to his flocks.

While this was happening, the Chancas, a neighboring tribe about sixty miles west of Cuzco, were arming for a war of expansion. Three months later they made their move, while Cuzco was still unprepared.

Hearing news of the approaching Chanca army, Cusi hurried back to Cuzco again to help defend it. But Viracocha, Urcon, and their close followers panicked, abandoned the capital, and fled to a fortress ten miles north. Cusi stepped into the vacuum and hurriedly rallied the people to brace for the assault. The Chancas stormed Cuzco but were pushed back. In a series of battles that followed, Cusi led the people of Cuzco to defeat the invaders.

Cusi offered the city back to his father, but the humiliated Viracocha had lost his taste for ruling and abdicated in favor of Urcon. However, accused of cowardice, Urcon was not acceptable to the people of Cuzco. Another of Cusi's brothers fought Urcon and killed him. By general acclamation Cusi was crowned the ninth Sapa Inca at the age of about twenty and received the name Pachacuti, "World Overturner" (or World Reformer), from the people he had rallied to save.

Pachacuti's first priority as emperor was reorganizing, rebuilding, and governing Cuzco. This he did for his first three years. A visionary urban planner, Pachacuti rebuilt Cuzco into a living reflection of Inca concepts of society and the universe. The new Cuzco was shaped like a puma, with its head the fortress of Sacsayhuaman and its heart the new Coricancha Sun Temple facing the great plaza. Pachacuti turned the course of two rivers so that they crossed the city, providing clean water. He greatly expanded the agricultural terrace system that sustained the economy. He built an astronomical observatory, the Ushnu. On the horizon he had forty-one high columns *(sekekuna)* erected, forming astronomical sight lines. These determined the solstices and other celestial events as sighted from the Coricancha Sun Temple in the city's heart. These sight lines also divided the city into administrative quadrants organized around different clans. He had other columns erected in the great plaza to determine the equinoxes.

Following Inca tradition, he married his sister Mama Anahuarque Coya. According to Guamán Poma, Mama Anahuarque "had a round face like his. She was beautiful, with small eyes and mouth. . . ." Like all Sapa Incas, he had children by many other women.

Pachacuti spent the next three years sojourning in other parts of the Inca realm. He returned to Cuzco determined to end the constant threat of warlike neighbors and bring security to his people. At the same time he felt chosen to fulfill Manco's vision of Inca destiny. He began the great project of his life: to spread and universalize the Inca way of life throughout the entire known world and to try to usher in an era of general peace, prosperity, and civilization.

THE LIFE OF PACHACUTI

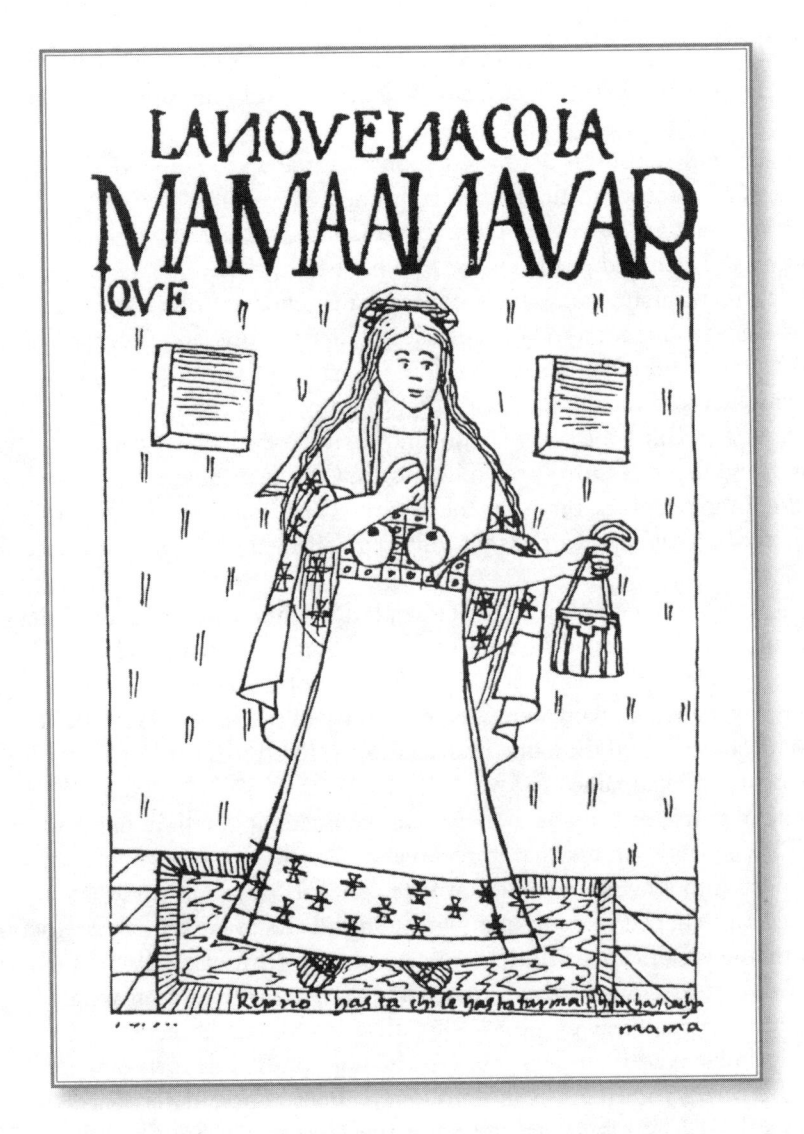

Anauarque. Poma de Ayala, Nueva crónica y buen gobierno.

Pachacuti tried to unify the empire through a vast cultural as well as administrative reorganization. Each of the conquered provinces had its own religious cult, based primarily on nature deities and local *wakakuna*. Pachacuti unified worship by emphasizing Wiracocha, the Creator, above and beyond all other deities. At the same time he did not interfere with each locality's traditions, since the Creator, as well as Earth Mother, Sun, Thunder, and Moon, were already part of their worship in various forms. He devised an official ceremonial round—of which the Situa was part—to be performed everywhere in Tawantinsuyu.

He began a three-year series of military sorties to expand the region of Inca domination, first to the northeast (Chinchasuyu), then to the east (Antisuyu). Much of the area was assimilated without serious warfare, as news had spread that acceptance of the

Inca system brought prosperity. For the following three years he visited the new parts of the realm, overseeing their reorganization and promulgating new laws while allowing each tribe to follow its ancient customs as long as they did not conflict with the new order. He permitted inheritance of land and organization of authority to vary according to the customs of each province. He tried to rationalize and harmonize the legal system throughout the empire, decreeing that many laws should be consistent throughout the realm. He made subject peoples into citizens. Pachacuti oversaw the building of roads, bridges, irrigation canals, farming terraces, temples, fortresses, palaces, and inns. He had storehouses erected in all the villages to put away supplies for years of need, when they would be distributed to all the people. He founded many new colonies in regions made fertile by Inca irrigation methods, instituting the system of *mitima*, through which he turned recalcitrant subject peoples into colonists in other areas. He expanded the system of *chasky* runners so that rapid communication could take place throughout Tawantinsuyu.

After that he left for more conquests in the Chinchasuyu, sending out his brother Capac and his heir Tupac Inca to conquer the coastal plains, then later directing them into Ecuador.

Badly in need of rest, Pachacuti decided to spend the next six years in peace, consolidation, and construction. He expanded the Inca school system (originally begun by his great grandfather Inca Roca). He turned Quechua (Runasimi) into a lingua franca, having it taught to all throughout the empire. He established terraced and irrigated fields everywhere and apportioned plots to each family according to their ability to work them. He set up a system of collective labor for both public and private works. The whole population was organized to till the public land (the fields of the deities and the Inca), as well as their own family plots. This was followed by sowing, harvesting, and storing. Widows, orphans, and the disabled were all cared for. He had the community build housing for all in need. A homeless person would make a request to the local council, which would appoint a day for the house to be built. The entire community would assemble and quickly complete the work. He established that every citizen should have a job, and fair compensation for it. He instituted holidays every month, daily markets in the towns and cities, and a regional fair every nine days so villagers and field workers could come to market (the first "weekends" on this continent). He had each province and city surveyed and their limits laid out. Around 1450 he began the construction of Machu Picchu.

Under Pachacuti's wise leadership from 1438 to 1471, the Empire of Tawantinsuyu succeeded in distributing the public wealth to suppress the scourges of hunger and economic misery throughout the realm. He knew that the Incas' greatest strength was not their army but their ability to improve general economic productivity by concentrating natural resources, organizing the work force, conserving the surplus product, and redistributing it in times of need. He did this over long distances and involving large numbers of people, without interfering with the traditional Andean system of mutual aid and clan *(ayllu)* relationships of reciprocity. On top of the traditional system, Pachacuti added the Inca institution of the *mita*, labor tax, through which all had to put in work in the fields of the Inca (the state) and the Sun. Through the system of redistribution, their *mita* work came back to the people. All benefited from the state infrastructure.

There were also injustices built into the Inca system, which could be rigid and authoritarian. The working people had little class mobility or personal freedom and bore the burden of the aristocracy. The system of *mitima* tore whole villages away from their ancestral roots and planted them in other regions. Subject tribes often revolted against Inca domination, preferring independence to the supposed advantages of civilization that the Incas thought they were bringing.

We have several conflicting accounts of Pachacuti's personality. Garcilaso El Inca writes glowingly, "Because of all [his accomplishments], his gracious disposition and mild rule, he was loved and worshipped as a second Jupiter . . . He lived in peace and tranquillity, as well obeyed as he was truly loved, and as well served as his goodness merited" (*Comentarios* Book 6, Chap. XXXIV; my translation).

However, Guamán Poma describes Pachacuti as meteoric: "a handsome tall man with a round face. When something angered him, his eyes became terrible like a puma's, and he lost all control." Poma goes on to say that Pachacuti drank and ate to excess, and when he went into one of his rages his sister-wife Mama Anahuarque Coya was afraid of him.

Another description of his personality is found in the great classical Quechua drama *Apu Ollantay*, a historical play with musical interludes by an unknown author, probably written in the 1490s. *Apu Ollantay* tells a story of love, punishment, and forgiveness. One of the main characters, the aging Pachacuti, near the end of his life, is portrayed as a stern defender of custom, law, and order.

In the play, Ollantay, one of Pachacuti's generals, is having a forbidden affair with the king's daughter, Cusi-Coyllur. Inca aristocrats were permitted to marry only other Incas, and Ollantay was from another tribe. In spite of this, Ollantay asks Pachacuti for permission to marry her. Pachacuti, the defender of conventional order, rejects him out of hand. Ollantay retreats with his tribal army to the fortress of Ollantaytambo, forty kilometers from Cuzco. Pachacuti, fearing a revolt, sends an Inca army after him. However, the rebel forces defeat the Inca army and Ollantay continues to hole up in his fortress. Meanwhile Pachacuti, in a rage, throws the pregnant Cusi-Coyllur in prison and gives her new baby daughter to the Virgins of the Sun to raise in the Sun Temple. At that point Pachacuti dies. The plot is resolved when Pachacuti's son Tupac, the new Inca, finally defeats Ollantay through a ruse, then forgives both him and Cusi-Coyllur, reunites the surprised couple with their daughter, and permits them to marry. Tupac appoints Ollantay governor of Cuzco while he himself marches off to war.

Despite the rigidity of his later years, Pachacuti was probably truly loved by most of his people, and he left an indelible mark on his civilization.

His death is described thus by the chronicler Sarmiento de Gamboa:

And then he called to the Incas Orejones of Cuzco, his relatives, and to Tupac Inca, his son, to whom in few words he spoke in this manner:

"Son . . . I leave you to these our relatives; they are now your fathers, so let them counsel you. Look after them, and they will serve you. When I am dead, take care of my body, and put it in my house Patallacta. Place my golden sculpture in the House of the Sun, and in all my subject provinces make the solemn sacrifices, and at the end perform the Purucaya feast, so I can go rest with my father the Sun."

And this finished, they say that he began to sing in a low and sad tone, in words of his tongue, that in Spanish sound like:

"Nací como lirio en el jardín, y así fuí criado, y como vino en mi edad, envejecí, y como había de morir, así me sequé y morí."

"As a lily in the garden
I was born,
and thus I was raised,
and as I came into my age,
I aged,
and since I had to die,
I dried out like this and died."

And having finished these words, he rested his head against a pillow and expired . . . (*Historia* Chap. XLVII; my translation)

SELECTED BIBLIOGRAPHY

THE FLOWER SONGS OF NEZAHUALCOYOTL
SOURCES AND TRANSLATIONS

Most of the surviving Nahuatl songs can be found in two major codices, *Romances de los señores de la Nueva España* and *Cantares mexicanos*. Both were compiled between 1560 and 1582. A few songs are duplicated in both the *Romances* and the *Cantares*, attesting to their authenticity and popularity. Neither manuscript has a compiler's name attached, though there is solid evidence of the identities of both.

The *Romances*, containing ten flower songs attributed to Nezahualcoyotl (or eleven, depending on how one counts), were probably collected by Juan Bautista Pomar, a great-grandson of Hungry Coyote. Although no scribe's name or date is on the only existing *Romances* manuscript, that manuscript was discovered bound together with Pomar's history of Texcoco, *Geographical Relation of Texcoco*, dated 1582. The two manuscripts are of the same vintage. Pomar wrote in his own language and for his own people to conserve their history, religion, and culture.

The *Cantares mexicanos*, with twenty-four to twenty-eight flower songs attributed to Nezahualcoyotl, was probably collected by the indigenous informants of Fray Bernardino de Sahagún as part of his great work known as the Florentine codex.

Since the Nahuas already had a written literary tradition before the Spaniards arrived, they learned the alphabet from the friars very quickly after their own ancient books were banned and burned. Soon many Nahuas could read and write in their own language, using the Spanish alphabet. Almost every Amerindian town appointed a notary to keep local records.

Two more of Hungry Coyote's songs are found in Spanish translation in *Historia chichimeca*, a history written in Spanish by Alva Ixtlilxochitl, another descendant of Hungry Coyote and surely an associate of Pomar. This book and *Relation of Texcoco* are the primary sources for Hungry Coyote's life and the history of his city-state, Texcoco. More of this history and a paraphrase of a Hungry Coyote poem have been passed down in *Monarquía indiana*, another contemporary codex by Fray Juan de Torquemada. The sacred hymns can be found in the Florentine codex, *Historia tolteca-chichimeca*, and *Anales de Cuauhtitlan*.

The quotes from Fray Diego Durán can be found in *Historia de las Indias de Nueva España* (1581), the first part translated into English as *The Aztecs: History of the Indies*, and the subsequent parts as *Book of the Gods and the Rites and the Ancient Calendar*.

There is no complete translation into English of the *Romances*. The best Spanish translations to date are still those by Garibay and León-Portilla. León-Portilla's beautiful English renderings of some of his Spanish translations are also excellent. Bierhorst's complete translation of the Cantares is precise and scholarly in many ways but also rife with interpretations of these poems as "ghost songs." In my own English translations I have used all of these works to try to find my way to understanding the originals.

Most of the songs in both the *Cantares* and the *Romances* have no titles, and in some instances several seem to be run together. For consistency and convenience in identifying the songs, I am retaining Garibay's song numbers for the *Romances* and Bierhorst's for the *Cantares*. The song numbers are followed by the manuscript pages where they can be found.

In the original manuscripts some of the songs contain stanzas apparently interjected by the singer at the time of compilation, usually addressed to Hungry Coyote. These have been omitted here. Also omitted are a few intrusions from Spanish.

Garibay's translations of most of the ancient songs into Spanish, along with commentaries, published over three decades beginning in 1937, changed the way ancient Nahuatl poetry was studied. His classic translations of the flower songs are still the standard against which all other translations must be judged. Yet another standard Nahuatl linguist and grammarian, J. Richard Andrews, could say about his work, "At times the Spanish translation is closer to invention than translation. . . ."

Translating poetry so difficult and arcane in the original, from a language so different from English, from texts so dense and intense, in which words placed together often mean something else, forces the translator to take liberties with the text. The Nahuatl texts are confusing in many places, the punctuation is inconsistent, and copyists' mistakes are so prevalent that all translators are called on to some extent to reconstruct the poems. There is ambiguity in numerous phrases, making one correct translation impossible. Because of the complex and contradictory nature of these songs, any coherent translation requires an interpretive point of view, making it open to valid criticism. That will always be the case in translations of the flower songs. Every translation is bound to be different, not only in shades of meaning but in omissions and inclusions. There will never be one definitive translation of most of these poems. The translator needs to cross vast linguistic and cultural gaps to obtain results that are understandable to the general reader.

The best modern biographies of Nezahualcoyotl are by J. L. Martínez (1972) and Frances Gillmor (1949).

THE FLOWER SONGS OF NEZAHUALCOYOTL
BIBLIOGRAPHY

Alva Ixtlilxochitl, Fernando de. *Obras históricas*. 2 vols. Mexico City: Universidad Nacional Autónoma de México, 1975-77.

Andrews, J. Richard. *Introduction to Classical Nahuatl*. Austin: University of Texas Press, 1975.

Aubin, J. M. A., ed. *Mapa Quinatzin. Anales del Museo*, primera época, vol. 2. Mexico: Museo Nacional de México, 1885.

Bierhorst, John, trans. *Cantares mexicanos: Songs of the Aztecs*. Stanford: Stanford University Press, 1985.

Cantares mexicanos. MS 1628 bis, Biblioteca Nacional, Mexico City.

Caso, Alfonso. *The Aztecs: People of the Sun*. Norman: University of Oklahoma Press, 1958.

Códice Chimalpopoca—Anales de Cuauhtitlán y leyenda de los soles. Translated by Primo Feliciano Velázquez. Mexico City: Universidad Nacional Autónoma de México, Instituto de Historia, Imprenta Universitaria, 1945.

Códice Xolotl. Edited by Charles E. Dibble. 2 vols. Mexico City: Publicaciones del Instituto de Historia, Primera serie, no. 22. Universidad Nacional Autónoma de México, 1951.

Durán, Diego. *The Aztecs: The History of the Indies of New Spain.* Translated by D. Heyden and F. Horcasitas. New York: Orion Press, 1964.

———. *Book of the Gods and the Rites and the Ancient Calendar.* Translated by F. Horcasitas and D. Heyden. Norman: University of Oklahoma Press, 1971.

Florentine codex, *see* Sahagún.

Garibay K., Ángel María. *Llave de nahuatl.* Mexico City: Editorial Porrúa, 1940.

———. *La literatura de los aztecas.* Mexico City: Joaquín Mortiz, 1964.

———. *Poesía náhuatl: Romances de los Señores de la Nueva España, Manuscrito de Juan Bautista de Pomar, Tezcoco, 1582.* 3 vols. Mexico City: Universidad Nacional Autónoma de México, 1964-68.

Gillmor, Frances. *Flute of the Smoking Mirror.* Albuquerque: University of New Mexico Press, 1949.

Hill, Jane H., and Kenneth C. Hill. *Speaking Mexicano.* Tucson: The University of Arizona Press, 1986.

Karttunen, Frances. *An Analytical Dictionary of Náhuatl.* Norman: University of Oklahoma Press, 1983.

Kissam, Edward, and Michael Schmidt, trans. *Poems of the Aztec Peoples.* Ypsilanti, Michigan: Bilingual Press/Editorial Bilingüe, 1983.

León-Portilla, Miguel. *The Broken Spears: The Aztec Account of the Conquest of Mexico.* Translated by L. Kemp. Boston: Beacon Press, 1962.

———. *Pre-Columbian Literatures of Mexico.* Norman: University of Oklahoma Press, 1969.

———. *Trece poetas del mundo azteca.* Mexico City: Universidad Nacional Autónoma de México, 1984.

———. *Fifteen Poets of the Aztec World.* Norman: University of Oklahoma Press, 1992.

Martínez, José L. *Nezahualcóyotl.* Mexico City: Fondo de Cultura Económica, 1972.

Molina, Alonso de. *Vocabulario en lengua castellana y mexicana y mexicana y castellana.* Mexico City: Editorial Porrúa, 1970.

Munguía Martínez, Jorge. *Introducción al estudio del idioma náhuatl.* Cuernavaca, Mexico: Asociación Cultural Mascarones, 1990.

Pomar, Juan Bautista de. *Relación de Pomar.* 1582. Edited by A. M. Garibay K. *Poesía nahuatl,* vol. 1. Mexico City: Universidad Nacional Autónoma de México, 1964.

Romances de los señores de la Nueva España. MS CDG-980 (G-59), University of Texas Library, Austin.

Sahagún, Bernardino de. *Códice florentino.* 3 vols. Mexico City: Secretaría de Gobernación, 1979.

———. *General History of the Things of New Spain* [Florentine codex]. Translated by A. J. O. Anderson and C. E. Dibble. Parts 1–13. Santa Fe, NM: American School of Research and Salt Lake City: University of Utah, 1950-82.

Soustelle, Jacques. *Daily Life of the Aztecs.* Stanford: Stanford University Press, 1961.

Torquemada, Juan de. *Monarchía indiana.* 5th ed. Mexico City: Editorial Porrúa, 1975.

THE SONGS OF DZITBALCHE
SOURCES AND TRANSLATIONS

In translating these texts I primarily referred to Barrera Vásquez's pioneering translation into Spanish (1965). I also referred to Munro S. Edmonson's English translation (1982), which is loosely based on Barrera Vásquez, but less literal.

Useful in understanding these texts is an acquaintance with the various *Books of Chilam Balam* (Barrera Vásquez 1948 and many other translations), the *Ritual of the Bacabs* (Roys 1965), the *Title of Calkini* (Barrera Vásquez 1957), and Fray Diego de Landa's *Relación de las cosas de Yucatán* (1959).

Other important Maya texts from Yucatan and Guatemala include the *Xiu Chronicle*, the *Chronicle of Chicxulub*, the *Title of Yaxkukul* (Restall 1998), the *Popol Vuh* (*Pop Wuj*) (Chávez 1979, Tedlock 1985, and many other translations), the *Annals of the Cakchiquels*, the *Title of the Lords of Totonicapán* (Recinos 1950, 1953), and the *Rabinal Achí* (Monterde 1979).

A good brief anthology of Mayan literature is *La literatura de los mayas* (Sodi 1964).

Standard dictionaries and grammars include *Diccionario de Motul Maya-Español* (Ciudad Real 1929), the *Diccionario Maya-Español, Español-Maya* (Barrera Vásquez et al. 1980), *Diccionario de elementos del maya yucateco colonial* (Swadesh 1991), and *A Maya Grammar* (Tozzer 1997).

THE SONGS OF DZITBALCHE
BIBLIOGRAPHY

Barrera Vásquez, Alfredo. *Códice de Calkini*. Campeche: Biblioteca Campechana, 1957.

———. *El libro de los cantares de Dzitbalché: Una traducción con notas y una introducción*. Mexico City: Instituto Nacional de Antropología e Historia, 1965.

Barrera Vásquez, Alfredo, and Silvia Rendón. *El libro de los libros de Chilam Balam*. Mexico City: Fondo de Cultura Económica, 1948.

Barrera Vásquez, Alfredo, et al. *Diccionario Maya-Español, Español-Maya*. Mérida, Mexico: Ediciones Cordemex, 1980. 2nd ed. Mexico City: Editorial Porrúa, 1991.

Chávez, Adrián I. *Pop Wuj*. Mexico City: Ediciones de la Casa Chata, 1979.

Ciudad Real, Antonio de. *Diccionario de Motul Maya-Español*. Mérida: Talleres de la Compañía Tipográfica Yucateca, 1929.

———. *Calepino maya de Motul*. 2 vols. Mexico City: Universidad Nacional Autónoma de México, 1984.

Craine, Eugene R., and Reginald C. Reindorp. *The Codex Pérez and the Book of Chilam Balam of Maní*. Norman: University of Oklahoma Press, 1979.

Edmonson, Munro S. "The Songs of Dzitbalché: A Literary Commentary." *Tlalocan* IX (1982): 173-208.

———. *The Ancient Future of the Itzás, The Book of Chilam Balam of Tizimin*. Austin: University of Texas Press, 1982.

Landa, Diego de. *Relación de las cosas de Yucatán*. [1556]. Mexico City: Editorial Porrúa, 1959.

———. *Yucatán Before and After the Conquest*. Translated by William Gates. Baltimore: The Maya Society, 1937. Reprint, New York: Dover, 1978.

Monterde, Francisco. *Teatro indígena prehispánico, Rabinal Achí*. Mexico City: Universidad Nacional Autónoma de México, 1979.

Recinos, Adrián. *Popol Vuh: The Sacred Book of the Ancient Quiché Maya*. Translated from Spanish by D. Goetz and S. G. Morley. Norman: University of Oklahoma Press, 1950.

———. *Annals of the Cakchiquels*. Translated from Spanish by D. Goetz. Norman: University of Oklahoma Press, 1953.

———. *Crónicas indígenas de Guatemala*. Guatemala: Academia de Geografía e Historia de Guatemala, 1957.

Recinos, Adrián, and Dionisio José Chonay. *Memorial de Sololá: Anales de los Cakchiqueles*. Mexico City: Fondo de Cultura Económica, 1950.

Recinos, Adrián, trans. *Popol Vuh*. Mexico City: Fondo de Cultura Económica, 1947.

Restall, Matthew. *Maya Conquistador*. [Includes translation of *Códice de Calkiní*.] Boston: Beacon Press, 1998.

Roys, Ralph L. *Ritual of the Bacabs*. Norman: University of Oklahoma Press, 1965.

———. *The Book of Chilam Balam of Chumayel*. Norman: University of Oklahoma Press, 1967.

Sodi M., Demetrio. *La literatura de los mayas*. Mexico City: Editorial Joaquín Mortiz, 1964.

Swadesh, Mauricio, M. Cristina Álvarez, and Juan R. Bastarrachea. *Diccionario de elementos del maya yucateco colonial*. Mexico City: Universidad Nacional Autónoma de México, 1991.

Tedlock, Dennis. *Popol Vuh*. New York: Simon & Schuster, 1985.

Tozzer, A. M. *A Maya Grammar*. Cambridge: Peabody Museum, 1921. Reprint, New York: Dover, 1977.

THE SACRED HYMNS OF PACHACUTI
SOURCES AND TRANSLATIONS

Pachacuti's hymns have come down to us in a manuscript entitled *Fábulas y ritos de los incas* (Fables and rites of the Incas), written between 1570 and 1584 by Cristóbal de Molina, priest of the hospital for native people in Cuzco. Some evidence suggests that Molina was a mestizo.

Although Molina seems to have known Quechua fluently, many lines in the hymns are confusing or unintelligible to both native Quechua speakers and scholars today. Quechua spelling was in its infancy at the time and very inconsistent. A variety of Quechua sounds do not exist in Spanish and most Spanish ears have difficulty distinguishing them (as do most English ears). Early chroniclers wrote those sounds in a variety of ways, since there was no ready place for them in the alphabet. Word division was inconsistent and could be arbitrary.

Furthermore, the only manuscript we have is a copy, probably made by someone who did not know Quechua and who easily might have copied many words incorrectly.

Molina gives his own translations into Spanish along with the Quechua originals, but these are sometimes loose and incomplete, so it is not always possible to correct the Quechua text from Molina's Spanish.

The first publication of Molina was an English version by Clements R. Markham in 1873, in which he simply translated Molina's Spanish translations into English. Since then a number of attempts have been made at reconstructing the poems in Quechua, with varying results, beginning with José Gregorio Castro (1921), followed by Juan A. Rozas (R. Rojas, 1937), J. M. B. Farfán Ayerbe (1945), Jesús Lara (1947, revised 1961), John Howland Rowe (1953), Teodoro L. Meneses (1964), and Henrique Urbano (Molina 1989).

I use a comparison of the original Molina with the Rozas, Lara, Rowe, and Urbano reconstructions as the basis for these translations, referring also to the other reconstructions and Spanish translations. I assume that the small variations between the repeated hymns are copyists' errors. The Quechua versions included here follow the Urbano reconstructions while retaining most of the paleography.

There are good biographies of Pachacuti by J. Imbelloni (1946) and M. Rostworowski de Díaz Canseco (1953).

For more information about the ancient Quechua literary world, one might start with *La poesía quechua* (1947) or *La literatura de los quechua* (1961), both by Jesús Lara.

The haillikuna of Manco Capac can be found in the work *The Antiquities of Perú* by Don Juan de Santa Cruz Pachacuti-Yamqui Salcamayhua, an indigenous Quechua, probably written about 1610 to 1620. Other important early sources of and about Inca poetry include the works of El Inca Garcilaso, Felipe Guamán Poma de Ayala, Fray Martín de Morúa, Pedro de Cieza de León, Pedro Sarmiento de Gamboa, Juan de Betanzos, and Francisco de Ávila.

THE SACRED HYMNS OF PACHACUTI
BIBLIOGRAPHY

Ascher, Marcia, and Robert Ascher. *Code of the Quipu: A Study in Media, Mathematics, and Culture.* Ann Arbor: University of Michigan Press, 1981.

Ávila, Francisco de, *Informaciones acerca de la religión y gobierno de los Incas.* [1590]. Lima: Sanmartí, 1918.

Betanzos, Juan de. *Suma y narración de los Incas.* [1576]. Cochabamba, Bolivia: Culturas Aborígenes de América, Fondo Rotatoria Editorial, 1992.

———. *Narrative of the Incas.* Translated by R. Hamilton and D. Buchanan. Austin: University of Texas Press, 1996.

Castro, José Gregorio. "Correcciones en la colección de libros y documentos referentes a la historia del Perú." *Revista Histórica,* tomo VII, entrega 1 (1921).

Cieza de León, Pedro de. *Obras completas.* 3 vols. Madrid: Consejo Superior de Investigaciones Científicas, Instituto Gonzalo Fernández de Oviedo, 1984-1985.

———. *The Incas of Pedro de Cieza de León.* Translated by H. de Onis. Norman: University of Oklahoma Press, 1959.

Farfán Ayerbe, J. M. B. "Oraciones reconstruidas de Cristóbal de Molina." *Revista del Museo Nacional* (1945): 72-76.

Garcilaso de la Vega, El Inca. *Comentarios reales de los incas.* [1609]. 2 vols. Lima: Fondo de Cultura Económica, 1991.

———. *Royal Commentaries of the Incas, Part One.* [1609]. Translated by H. V. Livermore. Austin: University of Texas Press, 1987.

Gutiérrez, Julio G., trans. *Ollantay.* Cuzco, Peru: Festival del Libro Cuzqueño, 1958.

Imbelloni, J. *Pachakuti IX: El incario crítico.* Buenos Aires: Editorial Humanior, 1946.

Lara, Jesús. *La poesía quechua*. Cochabamba, Bolivia: University Mayor de San Simón, 1947.

———. *La literatura de los quechua*. Cochabamba, Bolivia: Editorial Canelas, 1961.

———. *Diccionario qhëshwa-castellano, castellano-qhëshwa*. La Paz: Editorial "Los Amigos del Libro," 1978.

Ludeña de la Vega, Guillermo. *Nueva corónica y buen gobierno: La obra del cronista indio Felipe Guamán Poma de Ayala*. 2 vols. Lima: Editorial Nueva Educación, 1975.

Meneses, Teodoro L. *Himnos quechuas*. Lima: Universidad Nacional Mayor de San Marcos, 1964.

Molina, Cristóbal de. *Fábulas y ritos de los incas*. [1584]. Lima: Librería D. Miranda, 1943.

———. "An Account of the Fables and Rites of the Incas." In *Narratives of the Rites and Laws of the Yncas*. Translated by C. R. Markham. London: Hakluyt Society, 1873.

———. *Fábulas y mitos de los incas*. Translated by Henrique Urbano and Pierre Duviols. Madrid: Historia 16, 1989.

Morúa, Martín de. *Historia del orígen y genealogía real de los Reyes Incas del Perú*. Madrid: Consejo Superior de Investigaciones Científicas, Instituto Santo Toribio de Mogrovejo, 1946.

Pachacuti-Yamqui Salcamayhua, Don Juan de Santa Cruz. *Relación de antigüedades deste reyno de Pirú*. [1620]. Lima: Centro de Estudios Regionales Andinos "Bartolomé de Las Casas," 1993.

———. "An Account of the Antiquities of Peru." In *Narratives of the Rites and Laws of the Yncas*. Translated by C. R. Markham. London: Hakluyt Society, 1873.

Poma de Ayala, Felipe Guamán. *Letter to a King*. Translated by C. Dilke. New York: E. P. Dutton, 1978.

Rojas, Ricardo. *Himnos quechuas*. Buenos Aires: Instituto de Literatura Argentina, 1937.

Rostworowski de Díaz Canseco, María. *Pachacutec Inca Yupanqui*. Lima: Instituto de Estudios Peruanos, 1953.

Rowe, John Howland. "Eleven Inca Prayers from the Zithuvia Ritual." *Kroeber Anthropological Society, Papers*, VIII-IX (1953), pp. 82-99.

Sarmiento de Gamboa, Pedro. *Historia de los Incas*. [1572]. Buenos Aires: Emecé, 1943.

———. *History of the Incas*. Translated by C. R. Markham. London: Hakluyt Society, 1907.

Valera, Blas. *Relación de las costumbres antiguas de las naturales del Pirú*. [1590]. Mexico City: Secretaría de Educación Pública, 1956.